DEDICATION

I would like to dedicate this book to the boomer men in my life: my husband and my two brothers.

First, to my husband, William E. Lovett, Jr., who has demonstrated to me that it is possible after 40 to follow a dream and start a new, successful career. He has shown me that steadfast focus and unrelenting pursuit of a goal can be very rewarding for the boomer who wants to start over after 40. He has inspired my thoughts on why it is so necessary for the boomer who has the desire to make a career change to do it now—before it is too late.

Second, to my brother, A. Duncan Shirley, DMD, who astounds me daily by his ability to enjoy the present, finding humor in the smallest everyday happening and in the process creating memories for himself, his wife, and his five children. Without a lot of compulsive planning, he has pieced together a retirement plan that looks like it will work, though its method is unique and certainly not "by the book." He is a great example of what can be accomplished even without an early, before 40 focus on retirement planning.

Third, to my youngest brother, Norman D. Shirley, whose attention to every detail has paid off in spades as he approaches his 50s in good shape for retirement. A successful financial planner himself, he has practiced what he preached and it has worked.

With these three to inspire my thoughts, along with the hundreds of boomers with whom I've worked through these 18 years, I am convinced that some of the greatest people I have ever met are boomers.

They see possibilities no one else does, and as a group they are people who have changed every aspect of life as they have lived it. I believe boomers will continue to change behavioral patterns as they redefine ways to reach successful retirement and enjoy those ensuing golden years.

The BABY BOOMER FINANCIAL WAKE-UP CALL

It's Not Too Late to Be Financially Secure!

Kay R. Shirley, Ph.D., CFP

Dearborn
Financial Publishing, Inc.®

This publication is designed to provide accurate and authoritative information in regard to the subject matter covered. It is sold with the understanding that the publisher is not engaged in rendering legal, accounting, or other professional service. If legal advice or other expert assistance is required, the services of a competent professional person should be sought.

Editorial Director: Cynthia A. Zigmund
Managing Editor: Jack Kiburz
Interior Design: Lucy Jenkins
Cover Design: S. Laird Jenkins Corporation
Typesetting: the dotted i

Printed in the United States of America

99   00   01   10 9 8 7 6 5 4 3 2 1

Library of Congress Cataloging-in-Publication Data

Shirley, Kay R.
    The baby boomer financial wake-up call : it's not too late to be
financially secure / Kay R. Shirley
        p.   cm.
    Includes index.
    ISBN 0-7931-2970-2
    1. Baby boom generation—Finance, Personal.   2. Baby boom
generation—United States—Retirement.   3. Retirement income—United
States—Planning.   4. Investments—United States.   5. Retirees—
United States—Finance, Personal.   I. Title.
HG179.S4677   1999
332.024—dc21   98-31847
                                                                  CIP

ACKNOWLEDGMENTS

*T*his book would not have been possible without Beth Bassett, my invaluable research associate and editor. Beth re-energized me when I was tired and helped breathe life into my creativity when I was burned out. My heartfelt thanks to Beth.

Immense thanks to Jim Olsen, certified financial planner in Gretna, Louisiana, for generously offering the title of this book for my use. When he mentioned it, I loved it. And he gave it to me! He also contributed his thoughts, many of which are included in the text.

Cindy Zigmund, editorial director at Dearborn, was most helpful in thinking through the organization of the chapters, offering helpful ideas at every crucial juncture.

Thanks to Dani Cryssanthou, my publicist at Dearborn, whose enthusiasm about everything is so contagious that it affects every aspect of the creative process! She is great!

Stan Torgerson and John Bolton were most generous with their thoughts, time, and efforts in helping me understand various aspects of the aging process as it relates to boomers.

I am deeply grateful to my staff who faithfully attended to the needs of our wonderful clients, while I devoted my creative energies to the writing of this book. Special thanks to Jody Owenby, Anne Brady, Beth Lavender, Tiffany Rowell, Terri Thornton, and Lauren Clinard for helping with special research projects related to the development of the manuscript.

Many thanks to my clients whose life experiences formed the data from which the cases are created. I value their trust and friendship and have, therefore, changed all names and occupations to protect their privacy.

And last but not least, thanks to my husband, Billy, and to my parents, A.D. and Alma Shirley, who gave up private time and travel plans with me so I could finish this book.

CONTENTS

FOREWORD

*I*t dawned on me not long ago that my life could be radically different today if I had known 20 years ago what I know now. When I graduated from college in 1977, I was fortunate to have some money in the bank, albeit a modest amount. Although I wasn't a total prodigal, it never occurred to me to invest that money in anything beyond bank CDs, a new wardrobe, or another new car. (I had three new cars before the age of 25.)

I didn't know then that if I had put that money into a stock fund growing at about 10 percent per year, I would have the option of retiring today. I also didn't realize how quickly 20 years would pass.

Several years after the money I had in the bank had dwindled to nearly nothing, I met Kay Shirley. I was the editor of a business newspaper in Atlanta at the time, and Kay, a well-known financial planner in the city, had a story idea. She had worked with employees at two large companies in town, helping them to prepare for retirement. One company tended to pay a little better but encouraged its employees to live in prestigious neighborhoods, drive ritzy cars, and dress like Princess Di. The other company urged employees to sock away as much money as possible into its corporate stock. Guess which employees tended to retire earlier and wealthier?

It was a good story, but an even better lesson for a baby boomer like me who was steeped in the idea that the good life meant owning lots of stuff. Not long after that, my husband and I turned our savings over to Kay to invest in a smorgasbord of mutual funds. Her fundamental investment philosophy was one she espouses in the pages of this book: slow and steady wins the race.

She recommended that we invest a set amount each month, a system known as dollar cost averaging, so that even when the stock market turned down, we could benefit by buying more shares. I'm the bigger risk taker in my family, so Kay recommended that I spread some of my savings around in small stock funds and international equities but stay with a fund manager known to deliver acceptable returns through up and down markets.

When I left my position at the local paper to join the *Wall Street Journal,* I rolled my 401(k) money into a similar array of domestic and international funds, taking some risk but not too much. (*Wall Street Journal* reporters have to follow a stringent ethics code when it comes to buying and selling stocks.) Kay's program worked. Though at age 42 I'm not quite ready for early retirement, I do have options.

Actually, I don't think many people in my generation really yearn for early retirement—as in laying by the pool or hitting the links—the way our parents did. Our jobs tend to be more fulfilling, and if they're not, we have more alternatives to change careers or even work for ourselves. What many of us want instead of retirement is more control over our lives and more options. There's only one guaranteed way to get these things: have money in the bank.

In pursuit of these goals, Kay's advice has been a beacon of good sense for me. It's tempting when Wall Street has been in a prolonged bull market to try to swing for the fences with all your investments; it's also tempting to run for the hills when the market turns down. But as Kay counsels in her book, "The idea is to have good performance, but not peak performance, in your investments all year round. If you become impatient and are tempted to move your investments, it's like pulling up plants and replanting them at a different time of year. You could miss the blooming cycle for the plants you pulled up."

When my international stock funds were languishing in 1998, I suggested that we sell them and move into something performing a bit better. Kay told me she wasn't selling hers and recommended I hang on to mine as well. And as she notes in the book, "In 1998, the best opportunity was international, as it actually was in 1997, but only the very savvy investors had the nerve to take advantage of the opportunity. We tend to want to invest in the last good experience instead of looking for the next good experience."

Finding the next good experience, in the end, is the only way to build up your money in the bank and make sure you have options in your life.

—Anita Sharpe,
   Pulitzer Prize-winning journalist, *The Wall Street Journal*

PREFACE

*H*ere we are. The first year of the boomer generation. It's the class of '63's 35th reunion in Meridian, Mississippi. Truth be known, we are one year ahead of "official" boomers, but we like to claim we are a part of that generation. And, indeed, we are grateful for all who come after us—especially those of us who have invested well. Because if we invested early, those boomers after us will be investing, making the markets rise, and helping our funds grow!

As a class, we've done well financially. Perhaps it's because we were in the right place at the right time. Perhaps it's because we were well educated. Or perhaps we chose our professions wisely.

I like to think it's not only those things, but it's because we had a good foundation that was carefully laid in our high school and hometown relationships.

That foundation was solid—instilled in us by our parents, teachers, and clergy. It was based on straightforward direction and good, solid values. We were taught to work hard, do our best, never spend more than we made, always save for a rainy day, and invest at least some for retirement as soon as we got our first job.

Our foundation was supported by each of us supporting each other. We pretty much valued the same things and encouraged each other. And our friendships still carry us 35 years later. We had lots of worries—wondering what we were going to do on the weekend, loitering in the halls to talk, cutting class to eat at the drive-in.

Those were about the worst of our worries. But think what our students have to deal with today: guns and violent disruptions in school, not to mention academic standards that are lowered so that no one will fail. And employers like me wonder why the 38-year-old woman I just hired doesn't know how to convert a percent to a decimal—much less what it means. We wonder why 20- and 30-year-olds don't know how to spell. Apparently, they didn't enjoy the quality of education we did. Their teachers were obviously not as worried about the quality of education as ours were. They were probably worried about more threatening things— like attempts on their life.

We left high school and went our separate ways. We got jobs and started careers and families. Many of us began saving for retirement with our first jobs.

I really love what I do. Maybe coming to this career was luck. Maybe it was good parental guidance. I didn't start out to be a financial planner. I have moved through four careers in my working life, and at each succeeding career I learned something that would prepare me for the next step.

"Luck is where preparation meets opportunity!"

When I followed my parents' suggestion that in addition to a major in math I should also get a minor in education, I didn't really think I would ever teach. But when my husband was stationed at Fort Lee, Virginia, 30 years ago and I needed a job, I taught 8th grade math in Hopewell, Virginia.

Then I went to work at the Fort Lee Quartermaster School as a government employee and learned the importance of "completed staff work." The experience taught me how to "own" a project and take pride in its accuracy and completion—important principles that have helped me all through life.

When I moved to Atlanta to work with the Centers for Disease Control, still as a government employee, I was introduced to the field of instructional technology, which emphasizes the importance of linking learning with performance. I also gained an appreciation for the complexity of managing people in the workplace, an insight that prompted me to pursue and complete my doctorate in educational and business management with a minor in instructional technology.

Armed with a Ph.D., I became a management consultant in the aerospace engineering industry and to several medical schools where I was challenged (and paid well!) to help my clients improve managerial performance through the principles of systems engineering and performance-based instruction.

With the earnings from those endeavors, I invested with a stockbroker who converted my $100,000 to $90,000 in a year. After realizing he was not living in as nice a house as I was, was not driving as nice a car, was not as well educated, and was probably not as smart, I decided to learn how to manage my own money. He, by the way, is no longer a stockbroker!

That bad experience led me to believe there might be other people who shared my bad experience and needed to learn quickly and painlessly the investment principles I had learned. I began conducting seminars to teach what I had learned. Because I enjoyed it so much and it would not require me to travel, I decided to slowly wind down my management consulting practice and focus on building a financial-planning practice in Atlanta.

Today, after 18 years, I am pleased to say I am financially independent and I work because I want and love to, not because I have to. I didn't inherit any money; I just worked hard and saved the slow, steady way with small amounts invested in conservative, boring mutual funds I will discuss in Chapter 7.

I am one of many boomers who began early and are now approaching retirement financially secure. Through the 18 years I have been a financial planner, however, I have seen many other boomers who didn't start early; in fact, they may be 40 or 50 and have not yet started investing for retirement. They didn't spend less than they made; they didn't save for the rainy day; and they didn't invest for retirement early. So now as the first ones of the group enter their 50s, they are waking up to the reality that retirement is just around the corner and they find themselves behind the retirement investment curve. What are they to do? This book is written to help precisely those boomers.

If you are between the ages of 40 and 60 and have just started thinking about how you're going to retire securely, this book is for you. It will take you through the basics of investments to provide the crash course you need to map your retirement road. After you have completed reading the book and completing the worksheets, you will have a solid financial plan to achieve financial security.

You will find out what to do step-by-step and learn how others—starting with little or nothing in their boomer years—have made it. Chapters 2 through 5 address age-specific issues; Chapters 6 and 7 address the basics of retirement investing; Chapter 8 addresses the different types of tax-deferred accounts that will help you save taxes while investing for retirement; Chapters 9 and 10 discuss special problems facing boomers; and Chapter 11 contains the specific formula for becoming a millionaire if that's your goal.

As we plan for the future, it is often heartening to recall the past. Get off the treadmill for a few days and reflect. Many of us live in different places from the one where we grew up. I suppose we've all heard that you can't go home again. As appealing is it may be, we can't go back to those simpler times of apple pie and Chevrolet . . . Ozzie and Harriet, Roy Rogers, Andy Griffith, and Bonanza. Home again . . . maybe not, but why not try?

We can go back in our memories and recall the things we learned then that have helped us as we have moved through the years. Some things we may wish we had done differently. Unfortunately, we can't undo the past. And we can't roll back the clock. But we can make decisions today that will affect the rest of our life.

This book is written for those of you who never got started or got sidetracked somewhere along the way. Take the steps you need to take to secure your retirement. You still have time, even if you are just now waking up and starting late! You'll be glad you did!

The Baby Boomer's Dilemma

"A rising tide carries all ships."

*T*he end of World War II, greeted in this country with great relief and an outpouring of optimism, marked the beginning of a baby boom that lasted two decades. From 1946 to 1964, 76 million babies were born. To give you an idea of how significant that number is, let me give you an interesting comparison. From 1927 to 1945, there were 49 million babies born. To drive this point home: over this 19-year period, 49 million babies were born. During the next 19-year period, 76 million babies were born. Wouldn't you agree that's a baby boom! According to Robert J. Froehlich in *The Three Bears Are Dead!*, the impact of this huge group of babies cannot be looked at in isolation. There are "three separate and unprecedented demographic trends that are converging together to actually turn the United States upside down. These three trends are: a senior boom, a birth bust, and the aging of the baby boomers." Froehlich goes on to explain that

1

throughout all recorded history, only one in ten people could expect to live to the age of 65. Today, eight out of ten Americans will live past 65. . . . And just in case you think that this senior boom won't have an impact on certain industries in the stock market, remember this: the average age of the buyers of American made luxury cars is 65 and grandparents buy 40% of all the toys sold. Did you ever think that all those people with gray hair, driving around in a Cadillac with Toys 'R Us bags in the back might be sending you an investment message?

Second, consider the birth bust. Twenty percent of baby boomers will have no children at all and another 25 percent will have only one. Froehlich attributes the birth bust to our changing economic world. When we were an agricultural economy, it was important for parents to have cheap, available labor to help run the farm. What better source than your own children? Now, however, we have evolved to an industrial, information, and service economy. Children are no longer an asset; they actually are a liability—long-term cost with no economic return.

But what about the third trend: aging boomers? "Over ⅓ of all living Americans today is a baby boomer," Froehlich points out. When boomers arrived as infants, a thriving diaper and baby food industry was born along with a swelling of the ranks of pediatricians. Toddler baby boomers became the impetus behind the creation of a huge day care and kindergarten industry. When boomers entered elementary schools, new classrooms were built all across the nation. Between 1950 and 1975, the high-school population doubled, and the number of college students rose from 3.2 million in 1965 to 9 million in 1975.

Is it any wonder, when you think about it, that those 76 million teenagers made McDonald's and the whole fast-food industry so successful? Not to mention Levi's, Reebok, and Nike.

As boomers continued to age in the '70s and began buying their first homes, real estate prices appreciated as they never had before. Then in the '80s, boomers began to focus on self-improvement and career advancement. Consequently, pop psychology literature dealing with personal growth came into being and grew. The circulation of publications such as the *Wall Street Journal, Forbes,* and *Fortune* skyrocketed; CNN and CNBC came out of nowhere.

It doesn't take a genius to figure it out. If you can anticipate where the boomers are going, you can predict the future, says Froehlich. "Okay," he says, "now it's the '90s and guess what the boomer's #1 worry today is? . . . Retirement."

Boomers have now reached or will soon reach the middle of their life. The youngest are approaching 40. The oldest are slightly over 50. According to the Social Security Administration, 10 million baby boomers are going to live to age 90. Like it or not, a blueprint for financial security is the foundation on which any other plans must be built.

Specifically, boomers must ask:

- Have I been adequately funding my retirement?
- Will my preparations for retirement allow me to be as free from financial cares as I had hoped?
- Will I be financially independent?
- Will I have enough money to last for many years—maybe even until I reach age 100?
- How should I invest today to increase the likelihood that I will have enough money when I retire?
- When I retire, how should I invest to make sure I will have enough income growth to cover my cost of living as it increases with inflation?

Financial planning for retirement becomes even more important as expected life spans lengthen. And life expectancies *are* lengthening. In 1776 the average life expectancy was 35. A hundred years later, the life expectancy was only 40. A child born in 1997 can expect to live to be at least 76. "So," says Froehlich, "it took us 100 years from 1776 to 1876 to add an additional 5 years of life expectancy from 35 to 40. In the next 100 plus years, we have almost doubled the life expectancy from 40 to 76." Many boomers will outlive their parents. Some boomers will probably even live to 100. There may well be as many years (39) of retirement or semiretirement (61 through 100) as there were years of working (ages 22 through 60—38 years).

Some boomers have prepared well for the years ahead; others have not. It is the latter group I would like to address in this book. I would like to suggest a way boomers might create a secure financial future for themselves, whether they begin at 40 or at 50. First, however, let's examine some of the factors that have gone into making boomers who they are.

We are all products of our past: we are shaped by the times through which we have lived and by the parenting we received. But these influences reach further back and project far into the future, encompassing the times through which our parents lived and the parenting they received, and projecting into the future through our own children.

Boomers have been shaped by powerful forces, both contemporary and historically in the pasts of their parents and grandparents. Some outcomes of those shaping forces were positive; others have been decidedly negative.

Simply said, as we age we begin to see ourselves behave the way our parents did. As we have children, we begin to see ourselves in our children. So what role did our parents and grandparents play in shaping our future?

BOOMER PARENTS

"Just as the twig is bent, the tree's inclined."
—*Alexander Pope*

In my personal life and in my experience dealing with baby boomer clients, I have seen at least three parenting styles that seem generally to have led boomers to follow certain distinct patterns of behavior: styles that I call authoritarian parenting, laissez-faire parenting, and balanced parenting. The following analyses are, of course, broad generalizations.

Authoritarian Parenting

Some baby boomers grew up with parents who disciplined them strictly, largely because the boomers' grandparents had survived the Great Depression of the 1930s and were very uncompromising. Many of the people who lived through the extreme hardships of the Depression survived only through arduous work and frugality. As a result, they learned to value hard work, to appreciate whatever material goods they had, and to set uncompromising standards for themselves and their children.

The children of depression parents, who became parents of boomers, tended to perpetuate the kind of parenting they had received, and this parenting style was probably heightened by another historical event: World War II. Some parents of boomers, already reared with hard-and-fast rules, saw that to survive war the nation not only needed rules but needed to follow the rules. This led them to believe that their children needed to live by strict rules as well. Little tolerance was permitted for behavior that didn't adhere to the rules.

Some baby boomers followed the rules, either out of fear or out of respect, or, in some cases, through acts of early maturity. Unhappy in every way at home, others totally rebelled, violating all the rules, moving away from home, and living by their own rules. Some of these boomers were damaged permanently and lack the motivation and resources to change their circumstances in midlife.

Although I have no research to back my supposition, I believe many "flower children" of the '60s probably were a result of this type of parenting.

CASE IN POINT

A Flower Child at Midlife
(Suzanne)

"At the threshold of age 50, Suzanne has begun to wonder how much longer she can stand on her feet and cut hair."

A woman we will call Suzanne recently sought my advice about retirement planning, and her decision to seek financial help came none too soon. Suzanne is 48 years old. A former flower child (by her own admission), her life has been shaped by decisions made in early adulthood. As a teenager, she dropped out of school and ran away from home, seeking to escape the rules of strict parents. She lived at the home of one of her friends and refused to talk with her parents or to make any attempt to resolve her difficulties with them.

Instead of pursuing a college education, Suzanne became a hairdresser. Today, still a hairdresser, she is earning $40,000 a year and is a single mother with one 21-year-old son. Suzanne's feet and back hurt all the time because she works standing up all day every day.

At the threshold of age 50, Suzanne has begun to wonder how much longer she can stand on her feet and cut hair. She is, for the first time, thinking about saving for retirement. To do so, she must find enough motivation to embrace and maintain a rigorous regimen of saving and investing her savings wisely. She is among the boomers for whom this book is intended.

Laissez-Faire Parenting

At the far end of the spectrum of the parents of baby boomers were those who exerted little or no discipline, provided no direction, and adopted a laissez-faire attitude toward raising their children. Many of these parents probably were from well-to-do families in which the father may not have had to serve in World War II at all. Many of those parents partied and played golf while the hired help raised their children. They undoubtedly offered little advice and direction to their children, either through lack of ability to do so, lack of interest, or lack of time.

In the cases I have observed, parents of some boomers were reared by parents who themselves were successful business people and respected leaders in the community. Their successes were the result of hard work and an attention to detail. Their goal in life was to see that their children didn't have to work as hard as they had to have the same standard of living or the same respect in the community. Their life goal, it seemed, was to build businesses their children, who would become boomer parents, could inherit and run successfully without as much effort.

It seemed that boomers' parents, the children of depression parents, had it made. Their only job was to nurture the inherited businesses and pass them along. Many times it didn't prove to be that easy, however. The truth was that those parents of boomers hadn't developed the skills necessary to successfully carry on the trades their parents had understood so well. As a result, one of three things often happened:

Scenario one: Selling cheap.   Because boomers' parents had not provided the sweat equity that created their inherited businesses, they did not know or did not appreciate their real value. As a consequence, they sold the businesses for far less than they were worth.

Scenario two: Steady decline.   Lacking their own parents' know-how, imagination, and drive, boomers' parents simply continued to run the inherited businesses as their parents had. Unable to adjust to changing markets and business environments, they saw their businesses decline substantially.

Scenario three: Selling to boomers.   Some parents of boomers struggled with their inherited businesses and then gladly sold them to one of their children. But, like their parents, the children lacked the acumen to adjust to changing times.

Some of the boomers who eventually bought or inherited family businesses progressed well. Others tried but subsequently failed. Still others never bought or inherited the businesses at all and wouldn't have wanted them if they required work: what they had hoped for all along was an inheritance of money or investments that would support them during a lifetime of leisure.

By the time they reached college age, boomers in the third category were thoroughly conditioned to believe they would inherit their parents' estate and would never have to support themselves. Where was the need to exert oneself in the cause of accumulating wealth when wealth was theirs already? They had little thought for the future. Where was the need to plan for the future? The future was, after all, guaranteed. As a result, these boomers did not prepare themselves educationally to earn a living. They entrusted their futures to a single premise: they would inherit wealth.

CASE IN POINT
An Overprivileged Child at Midlife
(Robert)

*A*n astonishing truth had dawned on Robert: He would not inherit wealth; his parents were spending his inheritance.

Robert was a child expecting to inherit wealth, and he remembers his early years as lonely ones. Yes, he had brothers and sisters and friends and parents, but he felt lonely. His parents never once attended one of his school functions. PTA was out of the question.

He doesn't remember family vacations with his parents. He recalls his parents going away on golfing trips or cruises while he went away to summer camp. Robert's nanny raised him and she loved him. But she wasn't his mother.

Robert was often in the principal's office for some minor infraction. Psychologists today would hypothesize that Robert was attempting to capture his parents' attention. As a result, at 12 he was sent away to military school. College was not encouraged, but he went anyway. He took sociology and history courses, quitting just short of obtaining a degree and put to work in the family's successful furniture business. He married, had children, and began biding his time in the family business. Eventually, he grew weary of spending day after day doing work he did not enjoy and set out to find his future somewhere else.

There was little Robert was trained to do or motivated to do. He tried three other careers without success and at 46 came to see me. An astonishing truth had dawned on him: He would not inherit wealth; his parents were spending his inheritance.

In our discussions, he told me that his lack of early interest in retirement investing was due to a lack of parental guidance through the years. Not only was there no proactive guidance, but when his parents suggested that he save some of his earnings as a teenager, he was turned off because he saw his parents spending money like it was water. The lack of "guidance by example" touched other areas of his life as well. When his parents told him not to smoke, drink, or "party," he deliberately did it anyway because he saw his parents doing it. It was their failure to teach by example that he viewed as hypocrisy, so he categorically ignored any advice they tried to give him.

Robert, like Suzanne, has had an awakening at midlife, and he too will have to strive to make amends for years of financial drifting. Robert is among the boomers for whom this book is intended.

Balanced Parenting

One group of boomers' parents got it right. Often they were the ones who had lived through the depression with families that either lost everything or never had much to begin with. The parents of this group largely set out to help their children become equipped to survive in whatever the world ahead brought them. They gave career guidance and encouraged achievement. They did not want their children to become automatons, but they did explain that as long as personal integrity was not sacrificed, playing by the rules generally would be rewarded. Most of the rules by which society lives, they explained, rest on time-proven principles.

As a consequence, many boomers raised by these parents were exceptional achievers, responding well to incentives to climb the corporate ladder. They worked hard, married well, spent their money frugally, saved for the future, and tried to pass along those values to their own children.

CASE IN POINT

A High-Achieving Boomer

(George)

"Slow and steady wins the race."

As far back as 47-year-old George can remember, he worked, saved his money, and figured out how to earn more. When George was ten, his father got him a paper route. In the summer, George mowed yards and later worked packaging frozen corn-dogs in a nearby plant. When he reached high school, he learned how to buy old cars, repair them, and sell them to his friends for a profit. While his brother, two years older, spent his earnings, George saved.

When George graduated from high school, his parents insisted he go to college. It was a privilege they had not enjoyed. He had to help with his college expenses, but George didn't mind. He had been working for as long as he could remember.

George graduated with a general business degree at 22 and took a job with the local telephone company. Slowly, working at his management intern job, George began to move up the corporate ladder. Along the way, he married Mary, a telephone operator working for the same company, who started her career right out of high school. When it became obvious that computers were the wave of the future, George went to night school and earned a master's degree in computer science. As it turned out, this additional education would serve him well.

After George had been with the telephone company for 23 years and Mary had been with the company for 27 years, they began to suspect they might lose their jobs in a wave of downsizing. As a result, Mary went to pharmacy school, and George found a job with a computer company that provided services for many telecommunications companies.

Today, at 47, George is on a fast track with the computer company. His income has doubled since he left his original company, he has over $600,000 invested for retirement as a result of the pension buy-out he exercised with his first company, and he is building another retirement fund through his current employer's 40l(k). In addition, he has stock options. Mary, also 47, is happy working as a pharmacy technician at a local Wal-Mart.

George's brother also has done well, but his financial future is a bit more precarious than George's. Dan worked hard to become a physician, and he has worked hard at his practice. Although he has made a great deal of money, he has spent a lot, too. After medical school, Dan had school loans to pay off and a family to support, and so was never really able to save much. But Dan and his family have enjoyed an above-average lifestyle, taking costly vacations and socializing at the country club. Dan's practice is now changing, and he has decided to sell out to a large health maintenance organization (HMO). He hopes the HMO will go public so he will reap some rewards he can use for retirement. Otherwise, Dan's chief assets as he approaches 50 are the building in which he had his medical practice and the land on which it stands. If the HMO stock plan falls through, he will have to fund his retirement with the eventual sale of the land and building as few medical school graduates are financially able to buy his practice these days.

George and Dan's parents, by the way, are doing well. They are living in Florida on Social Security income, and they are debt-free. They find satisfaction in the way both their sons have turned out. George, who started more slowly and saved more steadily, will be able to retire earlier and maybe better than Dan. But both will make it.

HOW BOOMERS HAVE BEEN SHAPED BY HISTORY

When boomers were growing up during the '50s and '60s, optimism was high in the United States. Unemployment was down and inflation was low. More and more people were moving to the suburbs and more owned homes than ever before. Women began to move into careers that formerly had been almost the sole purview of men. Television showed us an unlimited world of "goods" that could be ours. In our spiffy new cars, we could go anywhere we wanted. Our personal horizons seemed limitless and so did those of our nation. After all, we had been on the winning side of the most extensive war the world had ever seen, and then in a "giant leap," a man had actually set foot on the moon. We could do anything.

By the '70s, as the middle of the boomer generation graduated from college, it began to look more and more as if the optimism of the '50s and early '60s had been too pervasive. As the Viet Nam war ended and we moved into the early '70s, there was trouble at home, too. News began to seep out about corruption at the highest levels of government. Our vice president resigned, then our president. There was mounting evidence that our use of pollutants was poisoning our environment, and we began to realize that this beautiful, fertile planet we loved might be in danger.

> *"A recession is when your neighbor loses his job. A depression is when you lose yours."*
>
> —*Ronald Reagan*

Through the '70s, boomers faced a recession, and they faced an embargo on oil that produced long lines at gas pumps and curtailed the use of their cars. A wage freeze was initiated. By the end of the decade and a change in the national political administration, boomers saw and felt the ravages of inflation as interest rates skyrocketed and the rising cost of living left them looking twice at their checkbooks. They felt that Chicken Little pessimism might now be warranted: the sky seemed indeed to be falling.

Jaded Optimists: The Boomer View of Life

As a result of what turned out to be a huge swing of the pendulum, boomers entered adulthood with a curious combination of optimism and trepidation. Having known such highs in the '50s and early '60s, their hopes had a long way to fall as the late '60s and early '70s shattered their illusions. Then came another swing of the pendulum when a massive tax cut prompted an economic boom during the '80s, and boomers became confident once again.

But what went up came down another time. Hopes of many boomers were dashed again in the late '80s and '90s as companies began to down-size—firing even the brightest and best workers, and the oldest and most dependable workers. In the face of downsizing, boomers began to per-ceive that doing a good job was not enough and that just having a job, any job, often had to suffice.

The times through which boomers have lived have created in their generation an attitude unlike any that has gone before. Boomers are at the same time seekers of the good life and doubters that it really exists. Their natural optimism is tempered by a generous amount of skepticism; they are jaded optimists.

Boomers' appetites for pleasure are large. They love to play, love to travel, love to eat good food. They are not afraid to spend money as were their depression-era grandparents. Yet they harbor fears about the future. They are afraid they'll lose their jobs, afraid they can't pay for their chil-dren's education, and afraid they'll not be able to help their aging par-ents. They are afraid they cannot fund their own retirements and afraid that when they reach retirement age, Social Security will not be available.

Boomers and Money

Because of the times through which they have lived, money is an es-pecially hot-button issue for boomers, write Stephen M. Pollan and Mark Levine in *Surviving the Squeeze: the Baby Boomer's Guide to Financial Well-Being in the 1990s.* In fact, according to psychologists, Pollan and Levine write, money has become a "blank screen onto which [all of us] can project all of our fears, attributes, and characteristics. The only other blank screen is sexuality." But money is the top issue for boomers be-cause "for most boomers, sex doesn't have the same power as money."

Boomers therefore see money as the be-all and end-all. Enough money can buy things and services that make life easier (and reinforce optimism).

But more than anything else, boomers understand that money can buy freedom: freedom from chores and freedom from the pressures of work.

Boomers and Credit

> *"I will gladly pay you tomorrow for a hamburger today."*

A facet of boomers' complicated, love-hate relationship with money is a tendency to spend impulsively and buy on credit to have today what they want today. Jim Olsen, a boomer and a financial planner with Financial Associates in Gretna, Louisiana, thinks this tendency is rooted in the escalating inflation and interest rates boomers faced as young adults.

Because of escalating inflation in the mid '70s into the early '80s, Olsen writes, buying something in the here and now meant getting it for less than it would cost in the future. So boomers bought now and charged what they bought. But credit came at a high cost: most credit card rates were capped at 18 percent, while the prime lending rate got as high as 22 percent.

"Feathering our nests was now a lot more expensive," Olsen contends. "And to make temptation worse, consumer interest was tax deductible. So at the time, buying rapidly inflating assets, paying tax-deductible interest, and repaying principal with inflated dollars was actually a rational decision."

It was also a decision that fueled a harmful cycle. As Olsen notes:

> The more we bought, the more prices rose in sympathy with demand, and the more we feared further increases, so we bought even more. In fairly short order we had spent all the money we had and most of the money we would receive for the next several years.
>
> In typical Catch-22 fashion, as one problem nears solution, another arrives to fill the developing void. Inflation finally began to subside, but so did the raises we expected to get to make it easy for us to tote the note. . . . In time the logic behind the buying on credit evaporated, but that didn't stop us. The credit habit

was on us and that plastic monkey on our backs proved difficult to shake.

Why are problems of debt still occurring even among boomers? It's not just overspending, it's also under-saving. If saving comes first, you can spend it and not go broke, because you don't owe anybody. Yet as obvious as that is, many boomers are still running around with substantial loan balances—including loans against their 40l(k) assets—and no savings.

Borrowing in the United States through the Years

Americans once considered it unwise to either borrow or lend money, but that has changed. We are now, in fact, a nation of debtors. Take a look at these statistics showing the growth of credit card debt in the United States through the years.

Year	$ Per Person on Credit Cards
1940	$ 11
1950–60	100
1980	392
1990	629
1992	1,100
1995	1,500
1997	3,058
1998 April	2,870

Source: Parade Magazine poll, 1990; Consumer Research, February 1998; USA Today, May 12, 1998.

How Baby Boomers Have Affected Various Markets

The following list of top stocks for given years illustrates how the huge baby boom generation has affected the market at every point in its lifetime.

Year	Top-Performing Stock
1953	Gerber (manufacturer of baby food) up 100 percent from the previous year
1957	Wham-o (toy maker) up 900 percent from the previous year
1963	Capital Records—Beatles and the Monkees
1969	Levi Strauss—boomers in jeans
1970s	Residential real estate—boomers marry and buy first home
1980s	*Forbes* and *Wall Street Journal*—boomers focus on careers
1990s	Technology stocks—boomers a big part of the information technology revolution

Boomers: Captives of the Past?

We are shaped by our past. As we age, we begin to see ourselves behaving the way our parents did. As we have children, we begin to see ourselves in our children. Although times have changed, we tend to cling to the spending habits of the past.

Is it enough, then, just to shrug our shoulders and say, "I'm not responsible for my actions; that's just the way I was raised"? Is it enough to say, "I can't change long-standing spending habits"? Is it enough to say, "I can't change my future because I cannot change my past"? I don't think so. I believe that although we are shaped by our past, we are not captive to it.

The Baby Boomer's
Financial Wake-Up Call

*"Never send to know for whom the bell tolls.
It tolls for thee."*

—John Donne

*Y*our wake-up call is here. You have to deal with reality up close and personal whether you ever have before or not. The time has come.

You've blown out the candles on your 40th or 50th (or whatever year was the most painful for you) birthday cake, partied all weekend, and now you don't want to get out of bed. You dread starting another grueling week. So you begin to wonder how much longer you're going to have to do this. You drag yourself to the coffee pot determined to find out where you stand for retirement.

It could be a little crease in the corner of your eye or a silver thread among your gold or brown or black. Or you suddenly realize that your child is nearly as tall as you are. Maybe you wake up with the invitation to your dreaded 20th high school reunion. Maybe it came when you realized you've started to care more about how your feet *feel* than how they *look!* Or one day you realize that Christmas is here again when it seems like only yesterday it was

Christmas last! Whatever triggers the awakening, we each experience it: the day the light bulb comes on and we realize we are no longer a part of the younger generation. In fact, we're looking more and more like our parents and unavoidably marching toward the age we thought we'd never see: we're going on 65.

Maybe you woke up when you went through a divorce. Or maybe you've always been single but suddenly you came out of your fantasy world and realized there might never be anyone else to take care of you but you. Maybe you're married, but one day you simply realized that your spouse would never make enough money to invest for retirement—and that it was all up to you.

Maybe your wake-up call came when you began to tally up how many dollars have flown through your checkbook in the past 20 years, and you asked yourself what you have to show for all that work and money.

When that awakening comes, we begin to perform two important tasks of midlife. We begin to assess what we've done with the part of life that has already been lived, and we begin to think about the future. Herein may lie a tremendous problem but also an opportunity. "[Midlife] can be a period of uncertainty and emotional strain," writes Wade C. Roof in *A Generation of Seekers: The Spiritual Journey of the Baby Boom Generation,* "but it can also be highly challenging and self-enriching. It is a time when adults experience a capacity for growth and maturity, which potentially can occur at any life stage but is especially likely at midlife."

In my 18 years as a financial adviser, I have known people who were 40- or 50-something and had carefully planned for later years; I have known people who made no preparation; and I have known those who had saved regularly and systematically through habit but had never thought about retirement or even counted up their dollars—but were ready when the time came.

Whatever our situation as we approach or advance through midlife, we have to deal with at least three broad categories of issues thrust upon us by the passage of years: mental issues, financial issues, and health issues.

BECOMING MENTALLY PREPARED
FOR THE REST OF YOUR LIFE

Someone once said, "If I'd known I was going to live this long, I would have

- saved more money,
- spent more time with my children,
- invested more time in developing friendships,
- spent more time with my parents,
- exercised more,
- taken more (or fewer) vacations, and
- _____(fill in the blank)."

Youth is characterized by a feeling of invulnerability and the denial of limitations and death. This phase of our life lasts longer than we think, according to John Bolton, Atlanta pastoral psychotherapist. It can go well into our thirties. For that period of time, we focus solely on the present in all areas of our life, including how we relate to money.

As our life lengthens, however, we begin to think not just about the present but also about the past and the future. We mentally assess the shortcomings of years gone by, as the list above shows, and maybe we resolve to do better in a future we now see will not be limitless, but finite.

And the time seems to move so quickly, much more quickly than when we were young. This illusion is due in part to the fact that each passing year actually represents a smaller and smaller proportion of the total life we have lived. For instance, when we are 5, one year is one-fifth (or 20 percent) of the total, but at 50, a year is only one-fiftieth (or 2 percent) of our total life.

Time seems to move swiftly for another reason: as we age, life becomes more routine with not as much variety. We get up and go to work, come home dead tired, slap some food on the table, eat with the TV blaring, get the kids to bed, and collapse ourselves, only to wake up and do it all over again the next day. We may become terribly tired of the routine, but we know we can't omit any steps. So much depends on the routine's faithful performance.

MIDLIFE CRISIS

"Adolescence is when you think you'll live forever.
Middle age is when you wonder how you've lasted
so long."

—*Anonymous*

Sometimes the passage of time and all it implies gets to be almost more than we can handle. We may wake up one day with a sense of futility and ask, "What am I doing?" "Is this all life is?" or "What is life all about, anyway?"

Central to the emergence of a period of midlife crisis is one thing, Bolton says: the realization that we are mortal. However, many critical events have preceded it, including those having to do with issues surrounding aging parents, aging children, and maturing careers. Throw in the fact that we are changing sexually and approaching the end of our reproductive lives, and you have a pressure cooker with the bobber bobbing pretty fast!!

In years past, the pressures of aging parents didn't exist, since most parents died in their late 60s or 70s. Now healthier living and medical advances are routinely extending lives well into the 80s and 90s, and most of us in midlife want to see that the last years of our parents' lives are lived as much as possible without stressful financial or emotional cares. I know I want to be as supportive of my parents as I possibly can, since all through my life they have been there for me. Those whose parents haven't been as supportive at least realize early childhood years took a chunk of time and money from their parents, so two to five years seems like a fair payback. For still others, guilt is the driving force for finding time and money to help parents.

Just as midlifers of the past largely escaped the pressures of aging parents, most had safely launched their children into independence by the time the parents were about 50, and they could then enjoy an empty nest, relax a bit, and travel some. However, because many boomers had their children later in life than was once the case, those children may still be around or still dependent as their parents live through midlife. In addition, many children today remain "in the nest" longer than was once the case.

CASE IN POINT

Boomers Finally Leaving Home
(Eric and Julie)

*I*t took Eric two years to find a job after he graduated from law school. For those two years, while he earned next to nothing at a bank, he lived with his mother and doctor father. During this time, Julie, Eric's sister, sustained two broken legs in an auto accident. She moved back home, and after an 18-month recovery period during which the insurance company made a financial settlement, Julie is now on her own and working. I recently saw Eric and Julie's mom, Ruth, who told me the great news that her children are doing fine now and the nest is empty.

The Ticking Biological Clock

An additional source of pressure for many boomer women is the fact that they have put off having children and then realize that their biological clocks have advanced beyond the point of no return. I remember well the mental depression I experienced at 38, when I realized I had waited too long to have children, and other career women have told me they went through the same empty feeling. It took a good two years before I accepted the fact that I had made choices earlier in my life and that I would never have a child. And, there was nothing I could do to change it now.

Changes Forced by Career Burnout

At the age of 45, my husband went through a similarly upsetting time when he burned out on his successful first career and decided to make a change. It took him four years and two test runs to find his new niche as a developer of retirement communities. But he and I both finally made our transition—though not without fear and pain. And you can, too.

The new-career approach works for many people who have tired of, and lost their enthusiasm for, first careers. Some go back to school to learn new skills. Some pursue dreams they had let go earlier in life. One man had always held inside jobs but through early retirement found a way to work in the outdoors he loves. Another man I know, who at 35 is going through his midlife crisis a bit early, wants to take a huge leap: he wants to quit his job and travel to Singapore to find work!

Changes Forced by the Search for a Meaningful Career

Other people make noble decisions about career changes. A survey by the Episcopal Church Pension Board in New York revealed that there are more ordained ministerial candidates over 40 than under. The Pension Board is concerned because these older ministers will have only 10 to 15 years of service and pension fund contributions before they are entitled to pensions.

Changes Forced by a Layoff

Some boomers fall into crisis at midlife when they are laid off from their jobs. Tommy, who had worked for the same company as an industrial engineer for 17 years, was one of those. When the company closed its plant, he was 46, had two children aged 15 and 13, and a wife earning about $30,000. Tommy was devastated over the loss of his job. He began shipping out résumés daily to companies similar to the one that had just closed the plant, looking for a job for the first time in his life. He had started working for a company when he was just out of college and after seven years was recruited by the company that had laid him off. To be without a job and to have to look for one was a frightening experience.

After three months Tommy's severance pay ran out, there were no job offers, and Tommy was sinking into a depression. Then a cousin in another city, who had faced a similar job loss about five years before, called him and began to brainstorm career ideas that would use Tommy's skills in a different environment. At his cousin's urging, Tommy began sending rewritten résumés to state and government-related organizations; within three weeks, he had a new job. The pay was less but adequate.

Symptoms of Midlife Crisis

If you are wondering if you are going through a midlife crisis, review the list below provided by counselor Bolton. If you are experiencing at least two of these symptoms you are very likely in such a crisis.

1. Increased dissatisfaction with many things in your life

2. Increased levels of irritation about small things and increased impatience

3. Loss of vision accompanied by a loss of optimism

4. An increased sense of how burdensome life is

5. A feeling of being trapped

6. A keen awareness of your own mortality

7. Fear of the future and a feeling of emptiness

8. A feeling of meaninglessness and a loss of purpose in life

People with poor recreational habits in particular don't know what to do with their time and may look into the future asking, "What's my life about?"

Suggestions for Coping with Midlife Crisis

Our passage from youth to middle age marks an important milestone in our life, but it is one that can cause inner turmoil. Perhaps we can best deal with that turmoil if we concentrate on putting our life in order so we can go on in a better way. Among the steps we should take toward this end are the following six:

1. Stop for a moment, be quiet, and think.

   "Learn to listen. Opportunity sometimes knocks very softly."
   —*Life's Little Instruction Book,* H. Jackson Brown, Jr.

2. Take stock of the past and set out to change the areas of your life that need adjustment. Mistakes happen. Unproductive or uncreative days happen. Everyone knows them. They are a part of real life, but don't get stuck in them.

"God has given us the faculties by which we are able to bear what comes to pass without being crushed or depressed thereby. Why then do we sit and moan and groan, blind to the Giver, making no acknowledgment to Him, but giving ourselves to complaints?"

—Epictetus

3. Make positive, definitive plans to bring about the changes you want.

   "Your work is to discover your work and then with all your heart to give yourself to it."

   —Buddha

4. Take the first step to implement your plan. Don't wait till everything is clear. Take action now.

   "Procrastination is the thief of time."

   —Edward Young

5. Don't lose faith if things don't happen quickly. Not everything can be done in a day. Be patient.

   Songwriter Hoagy Carmichael is supposed to have said:

   "Slow motion gets you there faster."

6. Remember to view your life holistically as a journey in which all parts are important and have their own unique pleasures.

   "Although all men have a common destiny, each individual also has to work out his personal salvation for himself.... We can help one another find out the meaning of life.... But in the last analysis, each is responsible for 'finding himself'."

   —Anonymous

FINANCIAL ISSUES

"I never been in no situation where havin' money made it any worse."

—Clinton Jones

While all the other issues exert pressure on boomers as they begin to wake up and realize that one day they will be 65, perhaps the one with the biggest punch is financial. The time eventually comes when the idealism of working at a job with low pay just because you enjoy it fades, and when spending to "create memories" at the expense of investing for retirement loses its glow. It is then that the retirement alarm clock begins to ring and the boomer springs into financial action. What needs to be done now? After all, I've never met anyone who wants to face retirement with a can of cat food on the table or the prospect of having to live with relatives. And the only way to avoid no food or housing is to have adequate money to support an independent lifestyle.

For some the wake-up call comes at 38; for others, at 42; for others, at 48; and for others it doesn't come until their 50s. Many factors influence the time the wake-up call comes. Suffice it to say—it *does* eventually come.

CASE IN POINT

A Boomer Couple Planning for Retirement
(Martha and Gene)

"With money in your pocket, you are wise, and you are handsome, and you sing well too."

—*Jewish proverb*

*M*artha came breezing into my office wearing the latest designer suit, a big diamond on her left hand, diamond pin on her jacket, and Ferragamo pumps. She looked like success. And success she was! She was the top real estate agent in the city with a healthy six-figure income to show for it! At 42, though, she had decided: no more jewelry, no more furs, no more new cars or furniture, no more new clothes—she needed to concentrate on retirement funding. "What are my options?" she asked. But she knew the answer.

The options were few and relatively simple:

1. Keep spending as she had up till now and work forever. Martha had read the book, *Die Broke,* by Stephen M. Pollan and Mark Levine, from which she had learned the secret to dying broke: "Quit [caring about your job] today, pay cash, and don't retire." They believe you should view your job as a source of money only. Develop no sense of loyalty toward your work—look only at the bottom line. Don't use credit for anything except your house and car. And never retire. They say: "I'm continually amazed at how obsessed people are with retirement. . . . First, because with all the obsessing, most of them are simply not going to be able to retire in the same manner as their parents. Second, because they're insane to even want to."

Martha was appalled. She did care about her work and wanted to care. She was ready to follow their advice about cutting up the credit cards. But she doesn't want to work forever and she fully intends to retire at least as well-off as her parents—better, she hopes. And if she is a prudent manager of her retirement funds, she won't die broke. But if she does, it won't be a big deal, either. Her goal is to have enough money to last her lifetime.

2. Slow down spending, invest for retirement, and quit work one day. This was an acceptable option for Martha because she had already slowed down her spending. She had $25,000 saved and ready to invest for retirement when she came in. But the third option was the one she chose.

3. Completely refocus and invest for retirement, drastically reducing spending. Martha was ready to completely refocus and invest for retirement. So her question was: "How much do I need to invest to support an annual lifestyle in today's dollars of $120,000 when I reach age 62?" If inflation continues at the average inflation recorded since 1926, the $120,000 needed will have to be 3 percent per year more to cover the inflated cost of living at her age 62. That is, Martha and Gene will need $216,733 a year when they're 62. To support that cost of living, their nest egg will have to be about $3 million. This nest egg will last for Martha's lifetime and be intact to leave to her daughter if she follows these two simple steps:

1. Invest the principal at a 10 percent compounded annual return.
2. Never spend all the return—leave at least enough in the account to allow the nest egg to grow to keep up with inflation.

Having been in real estate all her career, Martha knew how much she had made through the years. Recently she had totaled her earnings and found that since she had started work at age 22, she had earned $2,567,000. Sure, she had a nice home, fancy car, clothes, and jewelry to show for all that money. But two and a half million dollars is a lot of money and Martha had nothing saved toward retirement.

Her husband, Gene, a builder, had made a lot of money throughout his career, too. But as with lots of builders, he had lost a lot. And, like Martha, he didn't have anything saved for retirement. He had routinely used all his money for his next building project, each one larger than the one before. His plan was to sell off the last project and use the proceeds for retirement when he was ready.

And then a terrible thing happened they didn't expect. Gene was inspecting a deck that was 20 feet off the ground. He leaned on a rail he thought was secure and fell, breaking his hip and his leg in three places. He was lucky he didn't break his neck.

It would take Gene months, maybe a couple of years, to completely recover. So Martha decided to completely refocus. She felt she had no choice but to assume the lead in investing for retirement. She had decided to structure her thinking so that she would feel rewarded by seeing her retirement account grow instead of running to the mall to feel rewarded.

She and Gene had talked and decided they would be unable in retirement to maintain their current standard of living, which required an income in today's dollars of about $200,000 a year. They had decided to sell their $800,000 home and pay cash for a smaller home with the equity of about $350,000 in their existing home. They had decided to keep their car for at least ten years or 200,000 miles and buy a current model sports utility vehicle every 4 to 5 years leading up to and into retirement. This would represent a change from having a new car every 3 years.

Their plan would be to keep the $150,000 loan on their island home during retirement. Expensive trips would be eliminated, but that would happen naturally as Gene's accident would prevent them from taking their two ski trips every year. And until he recovered completely, his mobility would be severely limited anyway. Martha and Gene's recreation would have to be close to home.

Fortunately, their daughter, Stephanie, who had been living at home, had begun making her way in real estate by following in her mom's footsteps. She had just moved into her own home and was engaged to be married. After the wedding, expenses associated with Stephanie would be minimal.

The steps Martha and Gene planned to take would allow them to reduce their annual cost of living to $130,000 before taxes. So how much would Martha have to invest and how much would she need to earn on those investments to reach their goal?

Let's take a look at the numbers.

Cost of Living

	Current Monthly	*Retirement Monthly*
Home mortgage payment	$ 3,100	$ 0
Island home mortgage payment	729	729
Yard and general maintenance	300	200
Utilities	500	500
Real estate taxes	600	400
Food/eating out	1,000	1,000
Insurance (life)	250	100
Auto	600	400
Auto/homeowners insurance	350	350
Clothing	300	300
Vacations	300	800
Club/entertainment	1,200	1,000
Home improvements	300	300
Gifts	300	500
Charity	1,200	900
Personal necessities	500	500
Health insurance	400	600
Pension and profit sharing	2,500	0
Investments	950	0
Total	$ 15,379	$ 8,579
Total Annual	$184,548	$102,948

Tax Plan

	Current	Retirement
Income		
Net business income	$300,000	$0
Pension/profit-sharing plan	(30,000)	0
IRA income	0	$130,000
Total	$270,000	$130,000
Deductions		
Exemptions	($5,400)	($5,400)
Mortgage interest	(29,954)	(6,500)
Real estate taxes	(7,200)	(4,800)
Charity	(14,400)	(10,000)
State taxes	(11,846)	(5,486)
Total	($68,800)	($32,186)
Taxable Income	$201,200	$97,814
Taxes Owed		
Federal	($56,060)	($21,823)
State	(11,702)	(5,486)
Self-Employment (FICA)	(16,700)	0
Total	$84,462	$27,309
Income Analysis		
Total income	$300,000	$130,000
Less taxes	(84,462)	(27,309)
Less pension/profit-sharing plans	(30,000)	0
Income to Spend	$185,538	$102,691

At the time of this analysis, Martha was earning $300,000 a year. Because she is in real estate, she doesn't know how much she can expect to earn in upcoming years. She thinks her income will range between $300,000 and $350,000 but not quite reaching $350,000.

Remember that Martha has invested nothing for retirement until now when she's 42. If she invests 15 percent of her income each year for the next 20 years until she reaches 62, she will have invested a total of $976,742. This assumes she'll earn between $300,000 and $330,000 a year for the next 20 years.

We recommend that she invest those dollars into mutual funds that have produced 12 percent per year on average for the past 25 years—including the two very bad years of 1973 and 1974, times when the S&P 500 index declined 40 percent. While there is no guarantee that 12 percent will be possible in the future, I feel there is a good likelihood it will be, based on the fact that the funds I will invest in are managed by a system of management—not by a star or a series of stars. (See Chapter 7 for a list of the funds that meet my criteria.)

Following this plan, Martha will have a retirement nest egg of $3,441,810 by age 62. She and Gene should have about $14,000 a year from Social Security. Because they were born after 1938, however, they will not be eligible for their full benefit until they reach 67.

HEALTH ISSUES IN LATER YEARS

According to Dr. Ronald Hoffman in *Intelligent Medicine: A Guide to Optimizing Health and Preventing Illness for the Baby-Boomer Generation,* "Once upon a time, some of us lived as if there were no tomorrow. But we were surprised when the birthdays kept coming, even though the Beatles made 'when I'm sixty-four' seem to be light years away. Most of us are still here, but no matter how we once felt about life and the future, we've all had to cope with changes."

Baby boomers, born in the peace and affluence of the '50s and '60s, once had every reason to believe that medicine would soon find a solution for all of humankind's ills. Those old scourges polio and diphtheria had been conquered by vaccines. New antibiotics had been developed and others certainly were on the way that would take care of most any illness we had. New surgical techniques had been perfected. There seemed no limit to what medical science could do.

Now, however, it is evident that health cannot always be bought for the price of a pill or operation. In fact, the very antibiotics that once worked miracles are now proving ineffective in many cases because of overuse both in humans and in animals. We are now learning that our food supply may in fact be contributing to the problem because chickens, pigs, and cattle are routinely given massive doses of antibiotics as a preventive measure.

Moreover, as quickly as research eradicates old diseases, new ones seem to come along, writes Dr. Hoffman in *Intelligent Medicine.* For example, when boomers were growing up, they had never heard of AIDS, Legionnaires' disease, Lyme disease, or chronic fatigue syndrome.

New Health Challenges for Boomers

The news is not so good on another front. Even as we rethink our over-reliance on medical science, we learn that good health is being threatened by many pressures and habits our parents never knew.

Living at a fast pace.   Our parents used to putter around the house on Saturday and rest and go to church on Sunday. Today many of us work Saturday, Sunday, and on holidays, and when we don't work those days, we hit the mall.

Getting to work.   Once America was a country of small towns and traffic was insignificant. Today, just getting to work in traffic is a job, and many people begin most days by flying to distant cities to work.

A stressful environment.   Today, noise levels are high in our world. We are almost constantly within earshot of radios, televisions, stereos, traffic, lawn mowers, and leaf blowers.

Television has brought violence occurring around the world into our living rooms, and the print media supply us with missing details.

We breathe microscopic bits of the man-made materials we wear and with which we decorate our homes and offices. Many of the products we use, such as laundry detergent and some makeup, contain potentially harmful chemicals.

Increasingly, we cut the trees in cities and towns and replace them with stretches of asphalt. Increasingly, strip shopping malls and subdivisions encroach on woodlands and farmlands.

Suspect diets.   Our food and water contain chemicals. Where our parents may have grown up eating unadulterated vegetables from the garden, we now eat foods that contain preservatives, artificial colors, and sweeteners. In order to remain slim, we try fad diets and foods.

Lack of exercise.   Where our parents may have performed jobs that allowed them to move throughout the day, we often sit or stand all day in virtually the same spot performing repetitive motions that stress our skeletal systems. In the evenings, we spend hour after motionless hour watching television.

MIDLIFE: A SEASON FOR BEGINNINGS

Although you may already have lived 40 or 50 years, you may have 40, 50, or more years ahead of you! You're probably going to live a long time! You may have bungled some aspects of your life during the first 40 or 50 years, but in most cases the mistakes can be turned around, and the lessons of the past can be invaluable. There is no teacher like experience.

Midlife can be, in fact, a season in which you can begin again.

SUGGESTED READING

Joyce and Gene Daoust, *40-30-30: Fat Burning Nutrition* (Del Mar, Calif.: Wharton Publishing, 1997)

Robert C. Atkins, M.D., *Dr. Atkins' New Diet Revolution* (New York: Avon Books, 1997)

Winifred Conkling, *Stopping Time: Natural Remedies to Reverse Aging* (New York: Island Books, 1997)

Andrew Weil, M.D., *Natural Health, Natural Medicine* (Shelburne, Vt.: Chapters Publishing, 1998)

Ronald L. Hoffman, M.D., *Intelligent Medicine: A Guide to Optimizing Health and Preventing Illness for the Baby-Boomer Generation* (New York: Fireside, 1997)

Checklist of Things to Do to Improve Your Health

"Good health and good sense are two great blessings."

—Latin proverb

Andrew Weil, M.D., author of numerous self-help books and a newsletter on integrative medicine, has a general medical practice that focuses on natural and preventive medicine. His suggestions include ways to cope with the health challenges we face today by modifying diet and lifestyle to build the immune system. All of these are helpful as we try to remain healthy.

1. **Adjust your lifestyle to accommodate time to rest.** Find at least a day during each week to rest. It would be better to find two days, but with today's hectic pace, most are doing well to find one. This is a time to do nothing—no shopping, no work—just reading, watching TV, working in your garden, or any other activity that brings you peace.

2. **Manage your environment.** If you begin looking, you will find, as I did, plenty of nontoxic products from which to choose. This was easy for me as I was already reading labels. Perhaps you, too, will find the changes in products easy to integrate once you become aware.

3. **Screen the foods you eat.** Just as you read labels for fat and carbohydrate content, look for preservatives, such as sulfites, that have been added. Buy meats that say "No Additives" or buy "free-range poultry." To cut down on "junk food," don't buy it. Learn about the dangers of a "no-fat" diet. A diet rich in carbohydrates and very low in fat can actually cause you to gain weight. If you haven't done so yet, read *40-30-30: Fat-Burning Nutrition* by Joyce and Gene Daoust. My conclusion after reading it: go back to the basics. We all need a balanced diet. Home economics 101 gave us the basic food groups. Pull out those dusty old textbooks and bone up on the basics. Eat foods that are nutrient rich—rich in vitamins, minerals, fiber, and protein. Boomer parents ate more nutritious diets. Buy organically grown foods unless you have the luxury of tending a vegetable garden. Eat sensibly. Then stop eating after you satisfy your hunger.

4. **Exercise is a must.** Regular and moderate exercise is good for the bones, heart, and immune system. According to Dr. Ronald

Hoffman, more and more studies confirm that by keeping you limber and strong, exercise may actually stretch out or delay the aging process.

Approach exercise sanely. Make it a regular, not an intermittent, habit. If you haven't been physically active, start gradually. Walking is a good form of exercise that can go with you as you age. And don't overlook the exercise benefits of ballroom dancing. The important thing is that you do something and do it regularly in a relaxed, not competitive, way.

Answering Your Financial Wake-Up Call at 40

"In three words I can sum up everything I've learned about life. It goes on."

—Robert Frost

*D*uring our 40s many of the illusions that have previously blurred our vision begin to fall away, and we begin to see more clearly than we ever have before. It's now we can see that we don't know all the answers. We've made mistakes in the past and we know we can and will in all likelihood make more in the future and pay a price for them. It's now we know we have limitations; there are things we simply cannot do. And it's now we know we are mortal; our aging bodies tell us so.

But we see, too, that while we are mortal, we probably will live many more years and we must now begin to lay plans for those years before it's too late. Prominent among the plans we must make are those for a solid financial foundation for our retirement years.

At this juncture many, if not most, boomers discern a startling fact: somehow the money they have made—and they have made a lot—has slipped away. "Where did it go?" they ask themselves, and the answer comes resounding back. You spent it! Or you made some investments that were highflyers and you lost it! And on top of that, you've gotten yourself into a lot of debt!

This is the time, writes Louisiana financial planner Jim Olsen, when we find ourselves "on the wrong side of the yuppie River Styx, staring at columns of red ink; struggling to recall where the stuff is we got in exchange for that impressive stack of IOUs." What to do? It's simple, he writes. Not easy, but simple: "If I'm gazing across a river and want to get to the other side, what do I do? SWIM. . . . That's obviously not easy, but it is simple, i.e., not complex. The reason the solution isn't easy, i.e. not difficult, is because it involves changing behavior. . . . [It involves] delayed gratification."

So you're on the wrong side of the River Styx, the Hades side, and you want to get back to the good side. It's possible, but it takes some doing. You've got to swim hard, and you've got to pick your route with care. A boomer at 40 has to proceed with more care than ever before. He or she will have to take advantage of every investment opportunity that will maximize tax savings and use well every available dollar. This is the time to invest aggressively but with good common sense.

IF YOU HAVEN'T YET ESTABLISHED A FIRM RETIREMENT PLAN

To get started at 40 with a retirement plan, here are steps to take:

1. Fill out the household and family expense worksheet in Appendix B. This is a simple (i.e., not complex) exercise but it takes time and discipline. In addition, it's boring. After all, who wants to spend several hours going through cancelled checks and credit card statements categorizing expenditures to learn where their money went for the past 12 months? I'll tell you who. The people who want to get a grip on where they need to start in order to retire securely. This exercise is designed to help you uncover your money's "disappearing act." Ever wonder where all that money you earned last year went? After you complete your household and family expense worksheet, you'll know.

Now you might think this is where I'm going to tell you to start cutting expenses. But my purpose is to show you how to establish the exact dollar amount you need for living costs. I obviously don't want you to have to cut your standard of living when you retire. Of course, there will be some expenses that will decline naturally, such as your contributions to a 401(k) or other tax-deferred retirement plan. You may be able to eliminate life insurance; lunches out will probably taper off; and you won't need a business wardrobe. But other expenses, such as for traveling and health insurance, might increase.

After you've completed the worksheet for your current cost of living, you should subtract the approximate costs of items that will go down and add in those that will go up to create your anticipated cost of living at retirement in today's dollars.

2. Figure out exactly how much money you have in savings and investments.   Don't include the value of such assets as cars, house, furniture, or any other item you will be using in retirement.

3. Now plug your figures from numbers 1 and 2 above into the retirement income calculator worksheet at the end of Chapter 4 that shows you how to calculate your retirement income.   Your results will give you a customized retirement income analysis and will tell you how much you now have to invest to reach your retirement goal.

4. Begin to work with the details of investing your money aggressively but with good common sense.   The rest of this book provides criteria for selecting particular investments that will allow you to reach your goals. In this chapter, I'll tell you about people in their 40s who are just getting started with their retirement funding and show you how their differing circumstances led them to a variety of solutions. You'll learn that in the end the combination of solutions you choose will have your own unique touch. My intent is to stimulate your thinking and challenge you to reach for the best you can achieve as you prudently and carefully take big, aggressive steps today toward your goal of financial independence!

Some Dos and Don'ts for Investing

- Don't buy penny stocks.

  This is not the time to buy penny stocks, that is, stocks that cost less than a dollar a share. Do invest in mutual funds that are aggressive but have a proven management system in bad as well as good markets. (See Chapter 7.)

- Don't invest in tax shelters.

  This is not the time to fall for the pitch from some faraway broker who is trying to sell you a tax shelter, perhaps some far-fetched oil exploration scheme by phone with promises that seem too good to be true. Do select investments in which tax benefits are available through companies with proven track records. Do work with your own financial planner and tax adviser on a solid tax plan to seriously evaluate various tax write-offs and/or tax credits appropriate for your situation. There are good oil-drilling and tax-credit programs available, but you must be very selective and work with someone who knows how to evaluate the available programs. (See tax-planning strategies in Chapter 8.)

- Don't invest in traditional insurance.

  This is not the time for boomers to sink lots of dollars into traditional insurance products. Do investigate the benefits—and risks—of variable life insurance products. Traditional insurance programs don't offer the aggressive investment subaccounts you need at this stage of life. Be careful in choosing a variable product by evaluating the subaccount managers with the same criteria you would use to select a good mutual fund, as you can roughly equate a subaccount with a mutual fund. Of course, some of your money must go to buy life insurance, but a large portion of your money will be placed into the subaccounts, so the rating of the insurance company is not as important as the experience of the subaccount manager. (See my chart that rates various life insurance vehicles as retirement planning vehicles in Chapter 6.)

- Do invest the maximum allowed in your 401(k) plan.

  This is not the time for you to invest only the amount your company matches in the 401(k) program. (However, if that's all you can do, invest at least that much.) It is far better to invest the absolute maximum your company will allow into its 401(k) program. For most programs this absolute maximum is 15 percent of your gross salary up to approximately $10,000 per year. This maximum amount is adjusted annually for inflation.

I call these pointers "dos and don'ts" because you're beginning late and can't waste a single dollar making a mistake. By the same token, at 40 you can't waste a single opportunity for a good return on each dollar available in every tax category—tax deferred before retirement, taxable before and after retirement, and tax-free at retirement. (See Chapter 8 for a discussion of strategies for tax-wise retirement investing.)

BOOMERS AT THE JOB CROSSROADS

At 40 your first goal is to figure out how to earn $40,000 a year if you're not already. To do this, you may have to assess the job you presently hold. Maybe you want to go into business for yourself or find another, better-paying job. Also, we tend to perform better at jobs for which we are well suited, so if you are unhappy where you are, now is the time to make a change.

Starting a New Career—Your Own Business

> "Money doesn't grow on trees; you've got to beat the
> bushes for it."
>
> —Anonymous

At 40, if your career is stale, if you are burned out with the sameness of the day-to-day routine, and if you have some entrepreneurial spirit, consider taking the "big step": striking out on your own. Begin cautiously if possible by working on your own business venture on the weekends and in the evenings for a taste of what it will be like. If you're married, you should not begin your new business without the full support of your spouse.

Any new business will require a tremendous amount of your time and may require some family financing. If possible, plan to begin your business after you have saved twice the amount of money you think you will need. Have enough money saved to cover your living expenses for at least six months. Don't give up your job until you can see the money from your new business flowing into your checkbook within six months. In other words, do your homework. Don't walk out on your job one day and then try to figure out how you're going to make it.

Buy some books on starting the type of business you would like to own and talk to others who have made the same move. They have a wealth of experience from which you can benefit. If you don't have capital, choose a business that won't take capital. Be a broker. Be a consultant. Find a service you can turn into a profit.

But remember, starting your own business is risky. Two-thirds of all new businesses fail in the first two years. It is probably best to develop a plan B in case you don't make it in business for yourself.

Finding Another, Better-Paying Job

Maybe entrepreneurship isn't your thing. But you are totally burned out and need more income. Find another job with another company! The job market is hot now for those with skills in computers, health care, and financial services, to name a few. If your skills are in demand you have no problem. If your skills are outdated, take some courses and come out updated. You will live to 100 (and if not, you'll certainly outlive your parents), so you have plenty of time. Invest in updating your skills *now.* Maybe, on the other hand, you want to learn a new, entirely different skill. There's no time like the present.

CASE IN POINT

A Boomer Going Back to School
(Paul)

When Paul and his wife came to see me, 48-year-old Paul had lost his job through a downsizing at the electric utility company where he had worked for 28 years, having begun there straight out of high school. Now Paul's wheels began to turn, and he glimpsed the possibility of realizing a long-held dream: being a basketball coach. Paul had never been to college, so he couldn't teach, but now, at 48, he decided to go. Paul and his wife sold their home and moved to a college town so he could become a full-time student and graduate with the degree he needed.

Paul shared with me something his dad had told him many years ago—something he had not listened to then. "Son," his father had said, "five years from now you will be five years older. You can be five years older with a new set of skills or you can be five years older with the same old set of skills. The choice is yours." His dad, now in his 80s, is thrilled that his son is finally getting his college degree.

Going back to school may be for you if you find yourself lacking the qualifications to pursue a career that will give you the earning power you need to fund your retirement goals. It may even be a career you can continue into retirement, thereby reducing the amount of retirement money you will need.

Staying in Your Present Job and Investing Aggressively

Maybe owning your own business doesn't give you a thrill. Maybe you don't want to learn a new skill. Maybe you just like things the way they are and you like leaving your work at work. But until now you've borrowed from your 401(k) for funding your child's college. You've borrowed against your home for a new deck, your cars, and your credit card purchases. You can barely make ends meet now. Here are some steps you must take:

- *Live below your means.*
  When you get a raise, don't buy a bigger house or a new car. Cut out the expensive vacations, purchases for your home, redecorating, gift-buying, and new clothes.
- *Pay off your debt.*
  And once it is paid off, cut up the plastic and don't let the debt rise again.

- *Invest tax-deferred dollars.*
  Examples of tax-deferred plans are: profit-sharing plans, pension plans, 401(k) plans, IRAs, IRA-SEPs (for the self-employed), and deferred compensation plans. (See Chapter 8 for an in-depth description of these plans.)
- *Invest after-tax dollars today to create tax-free or tax-advantaged dollars in the future.*
  Examples: Roth IRAs, variable life insurance contracts. (See Chapter 8 for more information on each of these.)
- *Invest aggressively for growth.*
  Place your 401(k) dollars into the aggressive growth and growth categories. Every available dollar should be invested for retirement.
- *Fund a Roth IRA.*
  Every married taxpayer whose adjusted gross income is under $150,000 (under $95,000 for a single taxpayer) should fund a Roth IRA. Married taxpayers cannot file separately and get around this rule. If you qualify for a Roth, you should fund one regardless of the tax bracket you anticipate at retirement because all the dollars you invest and all the growth will be withdrawn completely tax-free, and you won't have to take the money at 70½ if you'd rather not. (See Chapter 8 for a discussion of the variety of IRAs available today.)

CASE IN POINT

A Boomer Couple in Debt
(Henry and Janet)

*L*et's take an in-depth look at the finances of Janet and Henry, a boomer couple who fell into just the debt trap Jim Olsen describes: "staring at columns of red ink; struggling to recall where the stuff is we got in exchange for that impressive stack of IOUs." Henry, a 43-year-old working in marketing, came to see me alone. Janet, 36, had a day off from her teacher's assistant job at a church school kindergarten and took the opportunity to accompany her six-year-old's first-grade class on a field trip. Our first step was to take a look at Henry and Janet's numbers. They looked pretty good until we got to the loan balances, the credit card debt, and the monthly deficit. Here are the numbers we saw.

Gross Annual Income		Net Monthly Income	
Henry	$80,000	Henry	$3,510
Janet	5,100	Janet	639
Total	$85,100	Total	$4,149

Net Worth

Assets

Home	$210,000	
'90 Plymouth	1,500	
'96 van	20,000	
Personal property	50,000	
401(k)	125,000	
Pension lump sum	127,000	
Total		$533,500

Liabilities

Home mortgage	$138,000	
Van loan	20,000*	
401(k) loan	23,400	
Credit cards	27,400	
401(k) loan	5,400	
Total		$214,200
Net Worth		$319,300

*Payment: $416/month

HOUSEHOLD AND FAMILY EXPENSES

	Current Monthly Expenses	Monthly Expenses After Debt Restructuring
Home mortgage	$1,164*	$1,164
Second mortgage	0	302
Van	416	150
Utilities	414	414
Food	500	500

Auto expenses	120*	120*
Meals out	100	100
Day care	85	85
Church	100	100
Clothing and gifts	0**	250
Entertainment and vacations	300	200
College funds	80	80
Personal expenses	60	60
Subscriptions	15	15
Credit card payments	725	0
ATMs and miscellaneous	300	300
Total	$4,379	$3,840

*Includes Insurance
**Included in credit cards

Net Monthly Income	$4,149	$4,149
Monthly Expenses	(4,379)	(3,840)
Monthly Deficit/Surplus	($ 230)	$ 309

As you can see, Janet and Henry are currently running a deficit each month. They continue to run up the credit cards—never able to make a dent in the balances. After the debt is restructured, they will be in a positive cash flow situation.

> *"Habits are first cobwebs, then cables."*
>
> —*Anonymous*

How Janet and Henry got so deeply in debt. After we looked at Janet and Henry's numbers, we discussed how they got caught in the debt trap. Janet and Henry had always been big spenders, but for a long time it didn't seem to be a big deal. Each time the credit card wolf was at their door, Henry would earn a big commission and fend off disaster. In time, however, Henry's company, like many others, restructured its commission schedule, and both his overall potential income and his magical extra cash flow dropped. There were no more large sums of money to bail him out of debt just in the nick of time.

Then help came in another guise. Henry's company offered to pay him to relocate from Florida to Atlanta. He and Janet saw it as an opportunity to pay off the card balances one final time. They took the offer and vowed to keep their financial house in order forevermore. They did not, however, cut up the plastic menaces that had been their downfall.

Habits are hard to break. Without the credit card payments flowing out each month, Henry was able to raise his 40l(k) contributions to the maximum. Invested in an indexed stock fund, he and Janet also benefited enormously from the phenomenal stock market performance of 1995–1997. They saw the 401(k) balance growing, and, as they said, they "became falsely confident." They thought they were "rich." And since they were rich and had been "good"— not charging for a few months—what would be the harm in having some of the "things" they wanted and "deserved"?

Within two years, the credit card balances were exceeding $20,000 again. Without the commission income to bail him out, Henry used the larger of the 401(k) loans to pay off the credit cards and make a $5,000 down payment on a $20,000 van. The couple were okay again, but, you guessed it, they didn't cut up the credit cards. Now, two years later they are right back where they were.

How the past shadows the present.   How in the world did Henry and Janet get started on this debt cycle to begin with? Thinking back, Henry can recall that his father always had credit card balances. His dad had died at 60 of a heart attack, and Henry thinks it was the financial stress finally catching up with him. Fortunately, because his dad had some life insurance, his mom's financial condition is all right.

Janet's parents always had card balances, too. Janet's dad used to be, and sadly still is, forever picking up the meal tab when he goes out to eat with friends or family, and he was and still is big on gift buying. Henry said, "He likes to be 'the good guy.'"

Janet's parents are relatively young, but her father, 62, has emphysema and does not work. Her mom is 56 and works as a nurse to support herself and her husband. They have declared bankruptcy twice and may have to again. They lost their home and now live in an apartment but still haven't caught on. Consequently, they are in an unenviable position: their five children may someday have to support them as they have no retirement funds saved.

How Janet and Henry can ease their cash flow and tackle their credit card debt.   First, they must cut up their credit cards and agree to change their spending habits. Then they should restructure their debt.

We determined that Henry and Janet have $30,000 of available equity in their home. They should obtain a second mortgage and pay off their credit card balances of $27,400. The rest of the money should be placed into a money market account to cover emergencies so they won't be tempted to use the plastic again. They can structure the second mortgage to be paid off in 15 years. Their monthly second mortgage payments will then be $302 a month instead of the $725 they are now paying monthly to their credit card companies. Furthermore, the interest on the second mortgage will be tax deductible. (The reason I didn't recommend a home equity loan—even though the interest is also tax deductible—is because the payment is 1.50 percent of the unpaid balance, which would be $450 instead of $302; and these people need every available dollar for current cash flow.)

Under the debt restructured plan they will be able to pay an extra $40 a month on the second mortgage and thereby have the second mortgage paid off in 13 years.

Deciding whether to continue funding the prepaid college tuition program for their children.   Ever since their two children—Jackie, 6, and Karen, 4—were born, Janet and Henry have been paying on a prepaid college program with the state of Florida. They now have $2,600 invested for Jackie, and they are continuing to fund her program at the rate of $38 a month. They have $2,400 invested for Karen and are continuing to fund that at a rate of $42 a month. This program allows a child to attend a state college in Florida with tuition prepaid for 120 hours. If the child gets a scholarship, the parents get their money back with interest of about 7 percent. If the child doesn't attend college or goes to an out-of-state school, the parents get their money back with no interest.

It's a good plan for Floridians, but now Henry and Janet think they will remain in Georgia, and if they do, in all likelihood the girls will not want to go to school in Florida. If Janet and Henry discontinue the program now, they get back the money they have invested.

The questions we needed to answer were: If they withdraw the funds, where should they put the balance? How much should they continue funding through another vehicle for each girl?

To obtain the answers, we ran an education funding analysis, factoring in the $5,000 balance the couple plan to reposition ($2,600 for Jackie and $2,400 for Karen). We determined that Janet and Henry will need about $190 a month for Jackie and $170 a month for Karen—a total of $360 per month to fully fund four years of college for each daughter at $10,000 a year in today's dollars. We are assuming they will attend a state college and the $10,000 will include tuition, books, fees, and room and board each year. This assumption is based on the most recent College Board average state college cost analysis, and the program we used assumes the costs will increase 6 percent a year.

Because Janet and Henry are now funding $80 a month in the college account and restructuring their debt will free up an additional $170 a month, they will have available a total of $250 a month to apply toward the college funding account. While this won't completely fund the girls' education (because that would be $360 a month), it will go much further than the $80 a month they had been contributing. This is a big priority for them as Henry wants to retire before the girls are finished with college.

The balances in the prepaid tuition program ($5,000) in Florida should be withdrawn and invested in a good aggressive growth mutual fund. Henry and Janet can tolerate a bit of volatility, as they have a minimum of 12 years for the money to grow. (In 12 years Henry will be 56, the age at which he wants to retire. Also, the girls will be 17 and 19, with one already using her college money and the other ready to begin drawing on it.) I recommended a mutual fund managed by a company that uses a system to manage each of its funds. (See Chapter 7 for assistance in selecting a mutual fund.)

Fortunately, Henry and Janet have some money (from the prepaid tuition plan in Florida) with which to open each account. If they had had no balances to begin with, their outlay for college funding would be greater. The monthly amount needed can be computed by using the chart entitled "College Funding" in the last section of this chapter.

Beginning in 1998, with the $250 a month ($3,000 a year) our couple intend to lay aside toward college, they can do two things. First, they will be able to fund $500 a year into an Education IRA for each daughter. This type of IRA will grow tax deferred until the child attends college, at which time all the funds can be withdrawn without being subject to any income or penalty taxes. (See Chapter 8 for a discussion of Education IRAs.)

Second, the money they have to invest for each daughter in excess of $500 a year (i.e., $1,000) can be put into a custodial account under the Uniform Gifts to Minors Act (UGMA), which will be consistent with the legal form under which the existing funds are being held in Florida's program. They should fund $83.33 a month into each daughter's UGMA account and $41.66 a month into each Education IRA.

In sum, each daughter's college money will be in two types of accounts: an Education IRA and a custodial account under UGMA. Both types of accounts can be invested in a variety of investment alternatives, including certificates of deposit or mutual funds. We recommend an aggressive growth mutual fund for each account for each girl.

Henry's financial status if he pursues another business opportunity. Henry is convinced he has topped out at his current job. His only pay increases will be in the 3 to 5 percent a year range, which is average for all businesses. He is considering a business opportunity that will afford him the chance to buy into a franchise, and working for himself, he has the potential of unlimited income. He won't be able to buy into the franchise completely up front, but he has a partner who can put up the initial money required until Henry can get his 401(k) loans paid down, thus freeing up dollars he could borrow later to invest in his own business.

Further, Henry plans to sell his and Janet's nearly new van and buy an older, but reliable, car for much less, thereby reducing his auto payment to $150 a month. He wants to be prepared to make payments on a new 401(k) loan when he needs to invest in his business.

Fortunately, when he leaves his existing company, the company will allow him to roll over into his 401(k) a lump sum instead of taking a monthly annuity, making it possible to borrow more as he needs it for his business venture. His eventual goal will be to pay off all of his 401(k) loans and also own his own business.

> *"Take calculated risks. That is quite different from being rash."*
>
> —*George Patton*

A new risk as the only way out.   Henry's is a risky venture. In two years, Henry will have been 30 years with his company. He has to think about what he will lose in retirement funds if he leaves before he has reached the 30-year mark. If Henry's business does not succeed, he will be saddled with high debt against his retirement fund and home for many years.

However, he thinks he has no choice but to take several steps back so he can really move forward. At 43, he has lots of energy to devote to a new career and is excited about the prospects. He and Janet have determined they will not use college funds to pay credit card balances or to fund the new business. They also decided not to borrow any more money against Henry's 401(k) for any purpose except to fund the new business.

Wrap-up.   This is one of those situations every financial planner dreads. The person seeking your advice wants to hear whatever will support his or her decision, which has already been made and is not negotiable. That was the case with Henry. When he came to see me, he had already decided to quit his job and go into business for himself. He just wanted help with doing that the best way.

Henry is determined to make this second career work. He is also determined to retire at 56 because his father died at 60 and his grandfather at 62, both with heart attacks. He wants to make sure he will have some years of retirement in case he carries the "short-life" gene of the males in his family. But he is exercising faithfully and eating properly, hoping to beat the odds on life expectancy.

Henry has finally realized the debt problem must be solved by curtailing spending. He is concerned that Janet is still not committed to reducing spending. He is fearful that her parental influences are deep and far-reaching in her psyche. He plans to make sure she comes to all the future meetings with me.

The couple's only hope is to cooperate in reaching their goals. I am convinced that Henry has the will to be successful in his new business venture. I am hopeful that he will be ready to retire at 56. Henry thinks they will spend the same monthly amount in retirement they are spending now under the restructured debt. They would like to spend for travel the money they are spending on college now. When Henry turns 58 (two years after he retires), their second mortgage will be paid off and they will have an extra cash flow of $302 a month that will afford them a little extra money for "breathing room."

Here is the retirement income analysis:

Retirement monthly income	$4,149 × 12 months =	$49,788
Present value		$49,788
Future value (Inflation projection for 13 years is 3%)		$73,115
Add projected taxes (estimated)		$10,878
Total Future Value		$83,993

At 56, Henry and Janet will need about $1,200,000 in a retirement nest egg to provide the monthly income they'll need. I am going to use 12 percent per year return on the retirement investments as Ibbotson Associates reports the historical long-term rate of return has been 10.8 percent per year. My suggestion that 12 percent a year is reasonable is because several mutual funds are available whose net long-term performance (even including the second worst market downtrend of 1973–74) has averaged at least 12 percent a year.

Obviously, if Henry chooses an index fund, the assumption of 12 percent per year will be overly optimistic as index funds have only averaged 10.8 percent a year. Therefore, we are recommending that Henry and other boomers playing catch-up will need to search for managed mutual funds that are likely to produce average annual returns greater than 10.8 percent. These boomers need to take the extra time required to find funds that can help them play catch-up the fastest. (For a complete discussion of how to select a mutual fund that has produced 12 percent returns as a conservative esti-mate, see Chapter 7.) Now, let's see if Henry and Janet will have what they will need.

Retirement Capital Needs Analysis

Income Sources	Current Value	Future Value*
Pension lump sum	$127,000	
40l(k)	$125,000	
Total	$252,000	$1,099,600

*Returns are computed at 12% per year for 13 years.

Henry is counting on his new business to be worth at least $200,000 in 13 years to make up the additional $100,000 retire-ment capital the couple will need when he retires. We pointed out that Henry's reliance on his new business to produce that kind of nest egg is a huge unknown.

As an alternative to selling his business, and if his new business produces income, he plans to invest for retirement monthly. Sup-pose it takes him 3 years to get the business on its feet. He will have 10 years after his business is producing an adequate amount of in-come to invest for retirement from his new business's cash flow. He will need to invest about $430 a month to meet the shortfall. His fallback position is the second mortgage being paid off in 15 years, thus reducing the couple's monthly income needs.

If they do not invest the required amount, their choices will be to either reduce their cost of living or move their retirement date from age 56 to age 59½. In 16 years, at 59½, they will need $94,000 a year, requiring a nest egg of about $1,350,000. By then the $252,000 retirement fund invested at 12 percent a year will have grown to $1,545,000. This nest egg will produce $108,000 a year and will meet their needs.

CASE IN POINT

45-Year-Olds Just Starting to Invest for Retirement
(I.M. and Sue Starting)

*T*hese are real people, but let's call them I. M. and Sue Starting. They have spent everything they had made till now. There are no retirement savings. I. M. has been the sole support of the family and Sue has been an at-home mom. When their first child, Dana, now 20 and a junior in college, began college, Sue went back to work to help with cost-of-living and college expenses. She now earns $20,000 as a receptionist for a real estate company. I. M. has steadily gotten pay increases and now earns $45,000 a year. Sue and I. M. are both 45 years old. Their son, Ivan, is 18 and will start college in the fall.

Dana is attending a state college where the tuition is $6,000 a year. She works for her spending money as a resident assistant in her dorm and at the college bookstore. Occasionally, her parents send her some extra cash. Ivan will be attending the local vocational technical school and living at home until he gets his certificate in computer science. His costs are about $2,000 a year.

Let's take a look at their net worth, cost of living, and tax plan.

Net Worth

Assets

Savings account	$ 1,300	
Checking account	700	
Savings bonds	1,500	
Home	130,000	
'90 Nissan	7,000	
'89 Pick-up	5,000	
'88 Honda (Dana)	3,000	
'86 Honda (Ivan)	2,000	
Furnishings/Personal property	50,000	
Subtotal		$200,500

Liabilities

Home mortgage	$ 78,000	
Car loan	2,000	
Credit cards	2,000	
Subtotal		$ 82,000
Net Worth		$118,500

Cost of Living

	Current Monthly	Retirement Monthly
Home mortgage, taxes and insurance	$ 1,000	$ 200
Yard	50	50
Utilities	225	225
Food	400	300
Recreation and entertainment	100	300
Automobile payment, insurance, and gas	350	350
Medical	100	200
Donations	166	100
Gifts/Holidays	130	130
Savings/Investments	563	0
College expenses	666	0
Life insurance	100	0
Personal necessities	60	60
Clothing	200	150
Depreciating assets		
(Home fix-up/Furnishings)	50	100
Off-the-wall/Miscellaneous	240	240
Total Monthly	$ 4,400	$ 2,405
Total Annual Need	$52,800	$28,860

Tax Plan

Income

Salary (I. M.)	$45,000
Salary (Sue)	20,000
40l(k) (I. M.)	(6,750)
Total	$58,250

Deductions

Exemptions	$10,800
Itemized:	
Mortgage interest	$ 6,000
Charity	2,000
Real estate taxes	1,000
State income taxes	2,000
Subtotal	$11,000
Total Deductions	$21,800
Federal Taxes Owed	$ 5,468
State Taxes Owed	1,817
FICA	4,973
Total Taxes Owed	$12,258

After-Tax Cost-of-Living Analysis

Total income	$65,000
Less taxes	(12,258)
Less 401(k)	(6,750)
Total available	$45,992
Total needed	52,800
Shortfall	($ 6,808)

The Startings have a shortfall of $6,808 a year. When their car is paid off in about eight months, they will be only $3,208 a year short of what they need. This is a tight plan for them. Until their car is paid off, they decided to cut back on meals out, clothing, recreation, and entertainment. They will have to make their cars last until one child is out of college. They will be looking for financial aid to help with Dana's college funding for two years. They can pay back the approximate $5,200 to $5,500 total they will need to cover the two-year shortfall after Dana graduates.

This family realizes they cannot do it all. At least they cannot do it all at one time! For now they have to begin investing for retirement and pay for the necessities of life. The extras will have to wait until they have received pay increases or some of their necessary expenses have dropped. In two years, Dana will be out of college.

Wrap-up.   This couple will make it. By investing 15 percent of his income into his 401(k), I. M. will be investing $6,750 a year. His company matches his contributions 100 percent up to 6 percent of what he puts in; so the company puts in $2,700 a year. I. M.'s 40l(k) investment is $6,750 plus $2,700, which equals $9,450 a year, or $787.50 a month.

I. M. will have to choose the aggressive options in his plan to attempt to secure, hopefully, a 14 percent per year return. If he maintains his contribution level and the company match until he's 65, he'll have $1,024,668 in his retirement nest egg at age 65. If the couple withdraws 7 percent a year for living expenses, they will have, in future dollars, $72,564 a year, which is the equivalent of $40,177 a year in today's dollars.

Retirement Income Analysis

Gross retirement income (today's dollars)	$40,177
Estimated taxes	(6,960)
Net after-tax income available	$33,217
Estimated retirement cost of living	$28,860
Surplus Income	**$4,357**

We are assuming a worst-case scenario here as far as retirement contributing is concerned. We are assuming I. M. will receive no pay increases and that his wife will never be able to contribute to the retirement investments. However, they fully intend to invest Sue's total net income for retirement as soon as the children are out on their own.

ADVICE FOR CATCHING UP

If you're a 40-year-old boomer playing catch-up, you've got to exercise discipline to reach your goal of financial independence. Here are the most important points to remember:

- Invest at least 15 percent of your total income for retirement.
- Direct your retirement investments through a tax-deferred plan such as a 40l(k) or profit-sharing plan, or (if self-employed) through an IRA-SEP, even if your company doesn't match. For every dollar you invest tax deferred, Uncle Sam gives you back some tax dollars that

go directly into your retirement account. *Example:* If you are in the 28 percent federal tax bracket and 6 percent state income tax bracket, and you invest $300 before taxes into your 401(k), you save $102 in taxes. So your paycheck actually only goes down $198 ($300 less $102) but the entire $300 goes into your retirement account. In effect, Uncle Sam is funding $102 of your retirement contribution. If your company matches your contribution, you will have even more.

- Invest to earn at least 12 percent per year, a rate-of-return goal that will be key to your playing catch-up with your retirement funding faster.
- Assess your present job and if you are unhappy or feel your income potential is limited, don't waste any time. Make a change now. You will still have time for a 20-year career somewhere else. And do it right this time: start investing for retirement right away!
- If you dream of being a millionaire by age 65, study the chart in the next section, and make it your goal to invest whatever amount you will need to reach your dream. It *is* possible for you—even starting in your 40s.

So You Want to Be a Millionaire by 65!

Oh, to be a millionaire! It's what you want, and many things are now going your way that will allow you to focus on retirement. Your home is furnished, for example. You now see a car as a necessity instead of a status symbol, so you don't need a new one every three years. That saves you money. When you go shopping, you see fewer and fewer things you want. That saves you money. And your spouse decided to go back to work to pay college expenses for your children, so that's taken care of. You have no outstanding debt. Now let's see what it would take for you to realize your goal. How much do you need to invest and what return do you need to reach the million-dollar mark?

Here's an example derived from inspecting the chart below. If you want to retire 25 years after your current age of 40 and you believe you can achieve 12 percent per year return on your investments, you would need to invest $527 per month. Is this really possible?

Suppose you are earning $45,000 a year and investing 15 percent of your gross income before taxes through your 401(k) plan at work. You choose investments that have earned 12 percent per year and you satisfy yourself that past returns of 12 percent, while not guaranteed, are possible for you going forward. This plan will allow you to achieve your goal of $1 million by age 65.

Let's take a look at how much you would have left to spend after taxes and retirement investing at the 15 percent level. We will assume that you have been paying down your home mortgage, and your interest deduction is low. We are also assuming your children are out of the house, you're taking deductions for only two of you, and you're not itemizing deductions but taking the standard deduction of $7,100 available in 1998.

Tax Plan to Determine Spendable Income

	With a 401(k)	Without a 401(k)
Gross income	$45,000	$45,000
40l(k)	(6,750)	0
Federal taxes	(3,863)	(4,875)
State taxes	(1,545)	(1,950)
FICA	(2,926)	(2,926)
Net Income to Spend	$29,916	$35,249
Retirement Contribution Analysis		
Tax savings going to the plan	$1,417/year	$118.08/month
Out-of-pocket retirement contribution	$5,333/year	$444.42/month
Total Contribution	$6,750/year	$562.50/month

For $562.50 a month to go into your 40l(k) plan, you have to put only $444.42 in and Uncle Sam will give you $118.08 a month for your account, which represents a 21 percent return on your money ($118 divided by $562) just from tax savings alone. This is the reason financial planners urge you to invest the maximum amount possible into your tax-deductible plans whether your company matches your contribution or not. In effect, Uncle Sam matches your contribution!

Therefore, if you are 40, your children are grown and supporting themselves, you have no deductions except the standard deduction, and you are earning $45,000 a year, it is possible to invest enough for retirement to have $1 million by age 65. Your only job is to make sure you can live on $2,493 a month.

If you are 40 or 45, take a look at the chart below to see how much you would have to invest to reach $1 million by age 65. Selecting your investment return is critical. You'll notice that the greater returns require the lower amounts to invest. Remember, however, the higher returns also require greater risk tolerance.

Also be aware that index funds will perform almost exactly as the unmanaged index. (Index funds usually charge around .5 percent as an annual fee.) For example, the S&P 500 index will show you the approximate return you would have realized over the years, and any fund that is "indexed" to the S&P will produce those approximate results. Appendix A shows the average annual returns of the S&P 500 as well as other asset classes dating back to 1926. You'll see that the S&P 500 index has produced a 10.8 percent per year return on average.

Some mutual funds don't outperform the index, whereas a much smaller number do. Unless you have relatively large amounts of money to invest, you will have to catch up by finding better returns than those the index has provided in the past. (Refer to Chapter 7 to learn how to select mutual funds that can help you catch up faster.)

If you are 40 or 45, take a look at the chart below to see how much you would have to invest to reach the $1 million mark by age 65.

$1 Million by Age 65

Age	Investment Amount/Month	Investment Return
40	$ 747	10%/yr
	526	12%/yr
	366	14%/yr
45	1,306	10%/yr
	1,000	12%/yr
	760	14%/yr

For ages other than 40 and 45, check out this type of chart in Chapter 4.

COLLEGE FUNDING

One of the major concerns for many boomers in their 40s who began their families late is how to finance a college education for their children. This is a particularly stressful concern since 40-something-year-olds who had children late could be anticipating retirement when the children are still in college. Of course, the later you start building an education fund, the more will be required.

The figures here assume you'll be paying 100 percent of the costs for four years at a state university at $10,000 a year for each child. They also assume the cost of education will increase 6 percent a year from 1998 until your child completes his or her degree.

If you plan to send a child to a school whose cost is more than $10,000 in 1998 dollars, simply multiply the monthly amount needed by the percentage increase the higher college cost represents. *Example:* If the college you're considering costs $15,000 a year, that cost is 50 percent higher than the $10,000 amount on which the table is built, so you should multiply the monthly amount needed by 150 percent to determine how much you should invest. Alternatively, if you expect the cost to be $5,000 a year, use half the monthly amount.

Child's Age	Cost for Four Years	Monthly Amount Needed (10% rate of return)
1	$117,798	$ 162
2	111,131	171
3	104,840	181
4	98,906	192
5	93,307	204
6	88,026	218
7	83,043	233
8	78,343	250
9	73,908	269
10	69,725	291
11	65,778	317
12	62,055	348
13	58,542	386
14	55,229	433
15	52,102	492
16	49,153	571
17	46,371	682
18	43,746	1,054

Answering Your Financial Wake-Up Call at 50

*T*oday, when many people can expect to live to be 100, those who reach 50 may expect to live 50 more years. In view of this lengthening of life spans, we must revise our ideas about who is old. In *Age Wave,* published in 1989, author Ken Dychtwald proposes the following delineations for people aged 50 and beyond: 50 through 64—middle adulthood; 65 through 79—late adulthood; and 80—old age. People in middle adulthood—50 through 64—are at the high point of their adult life in many ways, he writes.

You're 50!

Surely, most 50-year-old boomers find a lot of satisfaction in reviewing their accomplishments. You're 50 and all in all you've done pretty well for yourself. You've certainly worked hard, climbed the

ladder at work, and earned a lot of money. You have a great marriage and
two wonderful children about to leave the nest . . . and you've earned a
lot of money through the years. You've been to some really nice places,
eaten at some great restaurants, created lots of memories with your family . . . and you've earned a lot of money through the years. But wait.
What do you have to show for all that money? What will you have to support you in retirement only 15 years away? One thing is for sure. You don't
have much time left before that big retirement step is taken. Precious little time if you compare it with the 25 years you've already worked.

IF YOU HAVEN'T YET ESTABLISHED A FIRM RETIREMENT PLAN . . .

If waking up at 40 with no retirement fund is bad, waking up at 50 in
that situation is downright scary. If you fit that description, you must take
several steps immediately. You must assess where you are financially and
where you need to go, and then you must institute some drastic measures
to reach your retirement goal. These are similar to the steps you would
take at age 40 as well, which I've outlined in Chapter 3. The following is
an abbreviated version of those steps:

1. Fill out the household and family expense worksheet in Appendix B.
Knowing where your money is going now is the first step. Anticipating
the changes in your cost of living at retirement is necessary but very difficult without precise numbers that quantify your current cost of living.

**2. Determine exactly how much money you have now saved for retire-
ment.**   This includes your 401(k), IRAs, mutual funds, stocks, bonds, annuities, and savings accounts. It does not include assets such as your
house, cars, furniture, or other items you'll be using when you retire.

**3. When you have completed numbers 1 and 2 above, plug your results
into the retirement income calculator at the end of this chapter.**   The resulting figure will tell you how much you now have to invest to reach
your retirement goal.

50+ WITH NO RETIREMENT PLAN: DRASTIC MEASURES NEEDED

It has been said that life is a series of compromises . . .
time versus money.

—Anonymous

Sometimes compromises involve money; other times, time. Sometimes you cut back on the time you spend with various people; other times you cut back on how much money you spend. Still other times you adjust the quality of what you buy to fit the available cash; and you create limited, but quality, time with your family and friends. Money and time are related.

Boomers have learned that money buys freedom—that is, free time. If you have money, you can hire someone to paint the house or mow the yard. If you don't, you'll be pushing the mower or swinging the brush yourself. I remember when my brother Norm was trying to decide if he wanted to tackle the addition of a deck and porch to his home or hire someone to do it. He observed that there was a time when he would be willing to take every evening and weekend to build it himself. But not now at 46 with a six-year-old son with whom he and Renee preferred to spend time.

There are times in your life when preserving your money means more to you than your time. So you don't mind using your time to build your deck, mow the grass, make your own gift items, or paint the living room. Later in your life, having time means more to you than the money, so you're willing to pay someone to do various chores.

At 50, with no or few retirement dollars set aside, money will have to mean more to you than paying someone else to do your chores. You will have to make financial compromises. Or you find bargains that fit your available cash. Cathy, who works for a department store, remarked, "I do get an employee discount, but I don't buy clothing unless it's marked down. I don't have to sacrifice quality, because I look for bargains to begin with."

You can't do it all—at least not all at the same time. So let's look at three areas in which you may have to compromise.

Reduce your cost of living and classify needs versus wants.   No one can or should tell you how to spend your money. This is a decision you must make for yourself. To begin making some cuts, however, you must first know where your money goes. As unpleasant as the task is, if you want to retire successfully and you are beginning at 50, you owe it to yourself to take the time to complete the household and family expense worksheet in Appendix B.

To do it right, pull out last year's canceled checks and credit card statements. Go through each one and place the expenditure in the proper category until you have accounted for roughly every dollar you spent last year. Then highlight in yellow the expenses that are for "needs." For example, your home mortgage payment is a need, your clothing (by the time you are 50) is largely a want. Some food will be a need but lots of it, including eating out, will be classified as a want. Items you identify as wants offer an opportunity to cut back. Other typical wants include gifts, vacations, entertainment, excessive cosmetics, purchases for your home, cable TV premium channels, the extra phone line, your cell phone, long-distance phone calls, utility bills, (adjust to a little warmer temperature in the summertime and a little cooler in the wintertime), too-frequent dry cleaning, and subscriptions (do you really read all those magazines?).

After you've identified which items are fulfilling needs versus wants, you're in a better position to make some hard decisions. If you want to be financially independent at 65, you will have to decide where to cut and then stick with it. Then use the dollars you cut to invest for retirement.

Invest more and better, and spend the fruit, not the tree!   Plant your investment seeds and keep the plants planted. Diversify asset classes and diversify tax treatment.

Now, as never before, is the time to invest every dollar you can find. Invest in fairly aggressive mutual funds, real estate investment trusts, and, if your income is high enough, apartments that qualify for government-defined affordable housing tax credits, thereby allowing you to invest some of your tax dollars.

Think of your investments as seedlings you plant. Plant seeds and keep them planted. Don't pull them up every quarter or even every year to try to get them to grow better somewhere else as in "cashing out of your mutual fund and buying another." Give them time to grow. There will be times when they will grow faster than others. Be prepared to ride out the cycles. You're planting now for a harvest when you retire.

When you do retire, you will be eating the fruit of your investment trees. You certainly won't cut up the trees and burn the wood (as in "spend the principal").

Diversify your asset classes. Make sure your mutual funds (selected by my criteria in Chapter 7) are diversified among U.S. and non-U.S. companies—small, medium, and large; value and growth.

Also diversify your tax treatment. Place your investments into three tax treatment classifications:

1. Investments on which you pay taxes on the reinvested dividends and capital gains *now,* such as mutual funds or other investment vehicles registered in your name only
2. Investments on which you pay taxes on the reinvested dividends and capital gains *at retirement,* such as 401(k) plans, pension and profit-sharing plans, traditional IRAs, and fixed and variable annuities
3. Investments on which you *never pay taxes* (if properly structured) on the reinvested dividends and capital gains, such as Roth IRAs and universal and variable universal life insurance policies (See Chapter 8 for a complete discussion.)

If necessary, postpone full retirement.   You may think and hope you can retire at 55. Then when you do your retirement income planning in the cold light of day, you find that the numbers just don't support your hope and you'll have to postpone your retirement date.

CASE IN POINT

A Couple Coping with an Unpleasant Surprise
(Tom and Peg)

*F*ive years ago, at 48, Peg lost her $45,000-a-year job in a companywide downsizing. Tom, 50, works for a body shop and earns $24,000 a year. After 23 years with the company, Peg had worked her way up to a good job and nice salary. She had planned to stay there until she could retire at age 65, draw her pension, and she and Tom would be set for life. Peg's salary combined with Tom's allowed them to live well, perhaps too well.

Never giving a thought to the fact that their $69,000-a-year in-come might not always be there, the couple spent without restraint on items for their home, their children, and themselves. Gradually their credit card debt climbed to more than $25,000. Then the un-thinkable happened—Peg's company downsized and Peg was forced to take an early retirement package.

She received a lump sum pension buyout of $45,000 and she had only $5,000 left in her 401(k) after repaying her loans. She received $30,000 as a severance package ($20,805 net after a 17 percent av-erage federal tax, 6 percent state tax, and 7.65 percent FICA). Here's what Peg and Tom's net worth looked like.

Peg and Tom's Net Worth

Assets

Severance receivable	$ 20,805*	
Company stock	3,600	
Lump sum pension	45,000	
401(k)	5,000	
Home	120,000	
Personal property	65,000	
Automobiles	23,000	
Time share	8,400	
Total Assets		**$290,805**

*Net after taxes

Liabilities

Mortgage	$ 99,000	
Loan for screened porch	7,500	
Van loan	7,400	
Time share	1,200	
Unpaid dental bill	900	
Charge cards	25,642	
Computer loan	3,000	
Total Liabilities		**$144,642**
Net Worth (assets minus liabilities)		**$146,163**

When Peg first came to see me, she didn't want to discuss how she was going to create income for living costs but wanted advice on where to invest her lump sum pension and 401(k). So we focused attention there. She said she wanted to invest her rollover for growth and not touch it until she was ready to retire "for good" at age 70.

We discussed her risk tolerance. She said she had been conservative but realized she must assume some risk of fluctuating principal if she wanted her money to grow enough for retirement. I asked her what she would consider a "good" rate of return. She didn't know. But she was sure if her money decreased more than 10 percent in one year, she would lose sleep. So we set a target rate of return of 10 percent a year.

Using the model for how a 50-year-old should invest for retirement at age 65 or beyond, I placed 50 percent of Peg's money in mutual funds providing growth only and 50 percent in funds providing income primarily and modest growth, making sure she had at least 60 to 70 percent of her invested dollars in domestic funds and the balance in foreign funds.

With her retirement money safely invested, Peg began to search for a new job. After three months, she became frightened when she realized she wouldn't be able to replace her former salary. It was only then that she was willing to seriously discuss debt reduction. Monthly cash flow was going to be a problem, so I wanted to explore ways to reduce Peg and Tom's monthly payments. Before she left her job, I had encouraged Peg to refinance her home mortgage to reduce the monthly payments from $1,250 to $950 and thus gain a cash flow of $300 a month. To further ease the monthly cash flow, we decided to use Peg's severance pay to pay off the following debts.

Allocation of Severance Pay

Liability	Amount of Payment	Amount Saved Monthly
Screened porch	$ 7,500	$ 158/mo
Computer loan	3,000	250/mo
Van loan	7,400	470/mo
Time share	1,200	220/mo
Total	$19,100	$1,098/mo
Balance of severance to be used as savings		$1,705

Peg and Tom's after-tax living costs (after the savings realized by the debt reductions) decreased to $3,400 a month. Here's how they shared the income responsibilities for the household: Tom's take-home pay was $1,500 a month, or $18,000 a year. Peg's income from her new job was $1,900 a month, or $22,800 a year. Peg had to earn $29,000 before taxes to net the $22,800 needed for her share of the household expenses. Now, five years after the couple put the plan in place, here's the update.

Five-year update.   The first year was bad. Much to her surprise, it took Peg a whole year to find a job. She had to dip into her retirement funds for living costs. The job she finally found required her to commute 40 miles each way. She was earning $35,000; in other words, more than the minimum $29,000. But then the next year, Tom was injured in an auto accident, and because his work requires lifting and physical labor, he was out of work for a full year.

During the year Peg was looking for a job, the couple dipped into their rollover IRA funds to cover the $22,800 they needed from Peg's earnings. To net the $22,800, they had to withdraw $34,000. Fortunately, Tom's accident did not occur until Peg already had a job.

During the year Tom was without a job, they once again dipped into the rollover account and withdrew the remaining balance of $24,500. Fortunately, they had received about 12 percent a year for the first two years, so even though they were withdrawing every month, the balance was not limited just to principal. And when they withdrew to cover Tom's lost income, they took it out monthly, leaving the balance to grow as long as possible. For the next three years they struggled to make ends meet on Peg's lower salary and Tom's salary. They learned the hard way how to live on less.

Wrap-up: The result of drastic measures.   Until they both experienced job losses from which they could not recover quickly, Peg and Tom refused to consider curtailing their spending. Over the past five years, I have seen a dramatic change in their spending behavior. They not only have learned how to say no to their children but they have learned how to say no to themselves. They are single-minded in investing for retirement now.

This last year they have both worked. Peg has gotten a better-paying job closer to home. She is now earning $38,000 a year. She began participating in the company's 401(k) plan after she and Tom both were working again, and she contributes 15 percent a year. The couple went to Consumer Credit Counseling (CCC), a state-run agency to help people deal with debt reduction, for help with their credit card debt. They were required to surrender their cards to CCC and to pay a fixed amount of $526 a month to the agency. CCC negotiated a fixed rate for the card balance, which will be almost paid off in five years. After five years, their credit card balances will be down to about $1,000 and their mortgage to about $93,000. They have no other debt.

Peg has about $20,000 in her 401(k). When Peg got her $38,000-a-year job last year, Peg and Tom started contributing $200 a month to a mutual fund; the balance is now $2,875. Peg is 53, and the couple plans to retire at Peg's age 67. As soon as the credit cards are paid off, they plan to contribute what had been their monthly payment of $526 to their mutual fund. They think their retirement cost of living will be $27,600 when Peg turns 67. Let's look at an analysis of their retirement income in 14 years when Peg will be 67.

Retirement Income Analysis

Annual after-tax budget if retired today	$27,600
Future annual after-tax budget if retired in 14 years	
(Future dollars calculated at 3% inflation)	$41,747
Taxes (estimated at 24% average)	10,019
Total Retirement Income Need	$51,766

Income Sources

Invested Assets	*Current Value*	*Future Value**
401(k)	$20,000	$97,700
Contributions	525/mo	229,100
Mutual fund	2,000	9,800
Contributions	400/mo	174,600
Roth IRAs	4,000/yr	145,100
Total Retirement Nest Egg		$656,300
Spending potential		× .07
Income to spend		$45,941
Social Security income (Peg)		9,600
Social Security income (Tom)		5,748
Total		$61,289

*Projected rate of return is 12% for the 14-year period

As you can see, if Peg and Tom stay with their plan and their investments maintain a 12 percent-a-year return, they will have more than enough income to retire comfortably when Peg is 67. And remember, they literally started with nothing when she was 50 and he was 52.

Peg had originally thought she would not be able to retire until age 70. But our analysis shows she will be able to do it at 67. Because both Tom and Peg were born after 1938, they will not be eligible for full benefits from Social Security until age 67. Therefore, age 67 is a good target retirement age for them.

STARTING OVER AT 50

Unfortunately, some 50-year-old boomers find themselves starting over because of divorce, bad career decisions, or bad investment decisions earlier in life. Mary got a divorce she didn't want at age 49 and was scared about planning for her retirement years on her own. Today, ten years after she began, Mary's is a success story. But she never thought it would be and she was doubtful every step along the way. Let's look at her situation and review the drastic measures she took.

CASE IN POINT

Starting Over at 50
(Mary and Mark)

*T*heir marriage was in trouble when Mary, a 49-year-old homemaker, and Mark, a 53-year-old doctor, came to see me ten years ago in 1988. They had three children: Trent, 23; Allen, 21; and Hope, 17. Trent was out on his own; Allen was in his last year of college; and Hope was a senior in high school.

Divorce wasn't Mary's idea, but coming to see me was. The couple had also decided to see a marriage counselor to try to put their marriage back together. But part of the counseling process was to evaluate their finances together and to see where each would be (with a focus on Mary's situation) if divorce became a reality.

Mark had paid Mary $2,000 per year for bookkeeping services associated with his practice for six years so she could fund an IRA. Together we assessed their financial situation. Take a look at the numbers proposed for Mary's share as compared with total holdings.

Net Worth

Assets	Before Divorce	Mary's Share
Fixed		
Checking (joint)	$ 300	$ 150
Money market (Mark)	13,775	2,787
Money market (Mary)	8,200	8,200
Total Fixed Assets	$ 22,275	$ 11,137
Invested		
Mutual funds	$ 2,700	2,700
Mountain lot	5,000	5,000
IRA (Mark)	16,000	0
IRA (Mary)	15,430	15,430
Profit-Sharing plan (Mark)	24,000	12,000
Total Invested Assets	$ 63,130	$ 35,130
Use:		
Home	190,000	190,000
Personal property	95,000	65,000
Dodge van	8,000	0
Mercedes auto	25,000	25,000
Medical practice	200,000	0
Total Use Assets	$518,000	$280,000
Total Assets	$603,405	$326,267
Liabilities		
Home mortgage*	$110,000	110,000
Mercedes loan	0	15,000
Credit cards	23,000	0
Total Liabilities	$133,000	$125,000

*Original Loan was for $130,000 at 7% for 15 years; payment $1,168 per month

Net Worth	$470,405	$201,267

Splitting up the assets.   Mary and Mark decided that if they divorced, Mary would receive the assets and liabilities shown under the heading "Mary's Share." This would fulfill their intent that all assets and liabilities of the marriage be shared equally. Mark would retain his medical practice as it was his livelihood. He would move into an apartment, keep the van, pay off the credit cards, and pay Mary alimony until she could receive Social Security. They had agreed to this settlement as being fair as Mary had participated in building the practice in the early years and since then had managed the children and the household.

At first glance, it looks as if Mary is starting over with $200,000 worth of assets. Technically, she is. But for retirement purposes, she is only starting with $35,130, which represents the total of her invested assets. The greatest portion of her assets are those she will be "using" both now and in retirement. In other words, she won't be selling her home or car to create a retirement nest egg that could be used to provide income. Mary knows she can't earn enough to add a substantial amount to the retirement nest egg, and she is terrified about how she will prepare for retirement. She plans to find a job.

Mary recalls those early years of starting Mark's medical practice before they had started their family. They had gotten married when Mary was 22 and just out of nursing school. Mark completed his residency when she was 24, and for the next two years they both worked in the practice to get it started and begin paying back the school loans. Those were years filled with long hours, and all the money went back into the practice. They truly built the practice together.

Mary was certainly entitled to a portion of the earnings from that practice until her age 62. The problem was: Could Mark solve his alcohol problem and continue to practice? She was truly at risk. He was too. But he could do something about it. Mary was totally dependent on Mark's ability to pull himself out of alcohol dependency so he could continue to practice medicine.

Mark had handled all the family finances through the years. But through those years, Mark found it increasingly difficult to make enough money to support all their expenses without incurring debt. Until they came to see me after 27 years of marriage, Mary had no idea they had debt and no idea they had very little saved for retirement. Not that she would have actually cared because Mark had always handled things and she thought he always would. After all, she sacrificed her career and helped him build his practice so he could support them both.

Mark had not handled his personal stress well at all. Mary had grown increasingly concerned through the years about Mark's drinking in the evening. But it was Mary's discovery that Mark was seriously in jeopardy of losing his license to practice medicine that prompted the marriage and financial counseling. Mark had managed to prevent Mary from finding out how his problem had affected his work until he was given a warning. It was then that he was told he would have to go through a special detox program for doctors that would last three months. Someone would have to run his practice and see his patients during those three months.

1988 Tax Plan for Mark and Mary Before the Divorce

Salary (Mary)	$ 2,000
Practice income (Mark)	83,500
Interest income	500
Profit-sharing plan	(9,000)
Total	$77,000
Deductions	
Exemptions	$ 9,750
Itemized deductions	17,950
Total	$27,700
Taxable income	$49,300
Taxes owed	
Federal	($9,937)
State	(2,588)
FICA	(3,443)
Total	$15,968

Income Analysis

Mark's income	$83,500
Less profit-sharing plan	(9,000)
Less taxes	(15,968)
Spendable Income	$58,532

Household and Family Expenses
1988—Joint Before the Divorce

Category	Current Monthly
Food/groceries	$ 150
Home mortgage (plus taxes and insurance)	1,168
Yard	75
Clothes	250
Utilities	290
New household purchases	50
Auto payments, insurance, maintenance	475
Entertainment/Vacations	350
Life insurance	383
Health insurance	366
Disability insurance	390
Household maintenance and repair	35
Donations	400
Medical expenses	75
Gifts	167
Family's personal expenses	100
Tuition	646
Lot	71
Monthly Estimate	$ 5,441
Annual Total	$65,292
Spendable income	$58,532
Actual expenses	(65,292)
Shortfall	($ 6,760)

You can see that Mary and Mark are spending about $6,700 a year more than they are making. Over the years, this overspending has led to their high credit card balances. The combination of stresses and communication problems between the partners led them to the conclusion with their counselor that their marriage could not be saved.

Mary and Mark were divorced in 1989. They remained in the same house until Mark completed the detox program and was able to practice medicine again. He then moved into an apartment and as his income was restored, he started paying Mary $30,000 a year alimony until she would turn 62, at which time she will receive Social Security income under Mark's Social Security contributions. This is possible because she was married to him for more than 20 years.

Divorce and the emotional fallout over finances. Mary was terrified. First of all, she was concerned about Mark's alcohol dependency and fearful that even after the detox program he might backslide.

While Mark was going through the detox program, he was able to work as an assistant under supervision so that he could earn about $3,000 per month. After he completed the detox program and was reinstated, he could conduct his practice on his own, thus bringing his income back up to the $85,000 level. But the first year he struggled and was unable to pay Mary any alimony at all. After that, however, he did well.

In fact, over the next ten years, Mark did well and was able to function at a high level of productivity and increase his income beyond his previous level—even to $150,000. This was the income level he had been able to achieve during the years he was not burdened with the alcohol problem and was the income assumed in determining the alimony Mary would receive.

Second, not having worked since the early days of their marriage, Mary didn't think she could even find work—especially with enough income to support herself. But she did find a job. In 1989, Mary began a job at a hospital earning $20,000 a year. It was not a great salary but it was a start. She was determined to get her income up to where she could invest the $30,000 a year alimony ($20,000 net after taxes) for her retirement. At first, she would have to use some of the alimony to support herself.

Take a look at her projected expenses after the divorce and her anticipated expenses on retirement.

Household and Family Expenses for Mary
1989—After the Divorce

	Current (monthly)	Retirement (monthly)
Home mortgage,* taxes, insurance	$795*	$795
Utilities	255	255
Food	150	150
Recreation/Entertainment	100	300
Auto payment, insurance, gas, maintenance	250	250
Medical	50	300
Personal necessities (hair, cosmetics, etc.)	75	75
Clothing	125	100
Donations/Gifts	150	50
Savings/Investments	350	0
Insurance (life, disability)	0	0
Depreciating assets (major purchases)	0	
"Off-the-wall" money–miscellaneous	50	50
Total	$ 2,350	$ 2,325
Total Annual	$28,200	$27,900

*Mary refinanced: $110,000, 30 years, 6.5%, payment $695

After the first three years, from 1991 to 1998, Mary stayed with her plan of investing $30,000 a year. In addition, her earned income has grown to $38,000 and she has carved out an additional $5,000 to $8,000 a year for retirement investing.

Remember that she started over at age 50 with annual earnings of $20,000 and $35,000 of invested assets. She was to receive alimony but not for a year while Mark rebuilt his practice. Take a look at where Mary is today.

Net Worth for Mary
1998

Assets

Fixed

Checking	$2,000
Savings	4,000

Fixed Annuity	7,451	
Subtotal		$13,451
Invested		
Stocks	$29,755	
Conservative Mutual Funds	283,960	
Aggressive Mutual Funds	32,056	
Variable annuity (growth and income)	83,936	
Variable annuity (growth only)	18,861	
International mutual funds	12,160	
Variable annuity (growth and income)	64,051	
IRA (conservative mutual funds)	35,327	
Subtotal		$560,106
Use		
Home	$200,000	
Personal Property	95,000	
'85 Mercedes	10,000	
Mountain Lot	5,000	
Subtotal		$310,000
Total Assets		$883,557
Liabilities		
Mortgage	$ 97,000	
Subtotal		$ 97,000
Net Worth (assets less liabilities)		$786,557

Emotions that affect investment decisions and returns. Mary had acted on my investment recommendations through the years. We began with $2,000 in a fixed annuity, as Mary was investing for the first time on her own and wanted lots of safety and security.

We also opened an account with a fund family managed by a team system into which Mary would be contributing monthly. We chose a blue chip fund whose performance had beat the unmanaged S&P 500 index by two percentage points since 1953, a high-quality bond fund, and a fund containing smaller and medium-sized companies for a smaller portion of her money. Both the blue chip and bond funds were very conservative, and the third fund was a bit more aggressive. After several years of investing in these three funds and reviewing their respective returns and risks, Mary decided she wanted to remove her money from the bond fund and move it to a globally diversified fund that offered more risk but also more return. She had decided at this stage of her investing life that bonds were too conservative for her.

Over the years, as Mary learned to tolerate volatility, she became more comfortable with opening accounts with other families of funds managed by systems. In exchange for the volatility, she hoped for at least one percentage point more return.

In addition, as her tax bracket crept up she became increasingly concerned about taxes. We stopped future contributions into mutual funds and opened a variable annuity account. The variable annuities provided growth that was tax deferred until after age 59½. Our selection of funds and variable annuities was based on these three criteria:

1. Track records existed since 1973 so we could inspect their performance in bad years.
2. Performance netted at least 12 percent a year on average.
3. The performance since 1973 was created by a "system" of managing the money, not by a series of people who may not be there in the future. (For a complete discussion of these criteria, see Chapter 7.)

Over the years, Mary's investments have returned more than 12 percent a year. In 1998 we find Mary working very hard and thinking about slowing down. She is still nervous about her money, but she is not scared. She has made it for ten years on her own and she sees her accounts growing. She now wants to work half-time to spend more time with her mom, who is 92. She also wants to take more vacations with her children.

She wants to retire "for good" at 62, when her alimony stops and her Social Security income begins. Mary thinks her retirement income needs will be about the same as her needs were for the past ten years with a few exceptions. The dollars she has been accustomed to saving will go to medical expenses and travel. Today, at 59, she wants to know if she will be able to retire "for good" at age 62.

Retirement planning.   Since the cost of living shown above reflects uninflated dollars, we need to inflate them to give Mary an accurate picture of her needs in future dollars, corrected for inflation when she's 62. Let's take a look at an analysis of Mary's retirement income in three years when she's 62.

Retirement Income Analysis

Income Needed

Annual after-tax budget if retired today	$25,500
Future annual after-tax budget if retired in 3 years	
(Future dollars calculated for 3% inflation)	$27,865
Plus taxes (estimated at 16% average)	4,458
Total Retirement Income Need	$32,323

Income Sources

Invested Assets	*Current Value*	*Future Value**
Stocks	$ 29,755	$ 41,804
Mutual funds	328,176	461,064
Variable annuities	166,848	234,409
IRAs	35,327	49,632
Fixed annuity	7,451	8,625
Total Retirement Nest Egg	$567,557	$795,534

*Returns are computed at 12% a year except for the fixed annuity, which is 5%.

Spending potential	× .07
Income to spend	$55,687
Social Security income	12,000
Total Income Available for Retirement	$67,687

Mary is in great shape to retire at 62. Between now and then, she won't have to contribute any additional dollars for her retirement, allowing her to cut back her work schedule and spend her alimony doing things with her mom and her children. She paid the price in her early 50s and it's now paying off.

WHEN HEALTH TAKES PRECEDENCE
OVER MONEY

While we can talk in general terms about what 50-year-olds should do to steady their financial boats, we must remember the many atypical situations that are exceptions to the general rules.

Sometimes a couple must plan for the lifetime care of a mentally handicapped adult child. Sometimes one spouse's parents have to move in with the boomer couple. Sometimes the single boomer who is financially on the right track falls in love with someone who is not. Sometimes a boomer is in debt so deeply at 50 that the boomer has to take major steps back before moving forward. Sometimes health issues override all other concerns. Such was the case with Karl and June, both in their early 50s, when they came to my office.

CASE IN POINT

A Couple Facing Issues of Health
(Karl and June)

*K*arl, an easygoing 54-year-old project manager with a large company, had been offered a very attractive lump sum buyout of his annual pension in the amount of $473,000. This was to be a one-time offer; if Karl didn't take the lump sum, he would have to wait till age 65 and take his pension of $34,000 a year that would include no cost-of-living increases. He and June would be on the dreaded "fixed-income" we hear so much about. Moreover, if Karl died first, his wife would receive only one-half of the pension, or $17,000 a year. On the surface, this would seem to be a no-brainer: Karl should of course take the very generous lump sum buyout. Or should he?

The problem was health insurance. June, at 53, was not in good health. She had successfully fought a battle with breast cancer for three years and was still under the quarterly care of her oncologist. She also had rheumatoid arthritis that had affected her hands and feet. The health benefits for active employees of Karl's company provided maximum benefits with no limit on hospital costs for the whole family. The health benefits for retired employees were much less. As a retiree, Karl would move to an 80/20 plan, so if June's cancer returned, the couple would have to absorb 20 percent of the costs, which could be quite significant.

The couple were at loggerheads. Convinced the lump sum was the best deal, Karl wanted to take it. He knew he would have to work nine more years somewhere (and he wasn't ready to retire completely, anyway), but he wanted to take a less demanding job. He was so burned out with corporate America, he just wanted out—even if it meant walking the floors at Wal-Mart or Home Depot for his next job. He wanted very much to take the lump sum.

June was terrified. She knew Karl would have a hard time replacing his $90,000-a-year income, and she knew they needed at least $72,000 to support their cost of living. Over the years, she had seen her husband procrastinate about many things she considered important, and it looked to her as if he might procrastinate about finding another job. The company was pressuring. He had been given six weeks to tell it whether he would take the offer. June was also concerned that even if Karl did find another job with health benefits, they would be subject to a preexisting condition clause and her cancerous condition would be excluded from the coverage.

So they sat in my office: he all excited about the lump sum offer, she terrified that she was going to be railroaded into agreeing to something that would not be good for both of them.

Factors impacting the decision.   First, June did have a say in what happened. Before a lump sum can be awarded to an employee, the spouse must sign an agreement acknowledging a waiver of his or her rights to the survivor pension. Under the laws governing pensions, a spouse is entitled to receive a survivor annuity when the employee dies. Each retiring employee signs a document requesting either a pension for his or her life only or for a reduced pension for his or her lifetime so as to secure one-half up to a full pension for the life of the spouse. The options for pension payouts vary by company. Generally speaking, however, the larger the pension a spouse receives for life, the smaller the pension the employee receives for life.

If a company gives employees the option of a lump sum instead of a monthly annuity, spouses must indicate in writing their agreement and understanding they will receive no annuity from the company when an employee dies. When the lump sum is rolled over to an IRA, a spouse must be named as the primary beneficiary on the account unless the spouse signs the beneficiary form specifically waiving the right to receive the proceeds of the account at the death of the account owner. The spouse therefore is only subject to the risk of the investments chosen by the employee for the rollover funds. Thus, no spouse can be forced into anything with which the spouse does not feel comfortable.

Many think a rollover account can be held in a joint name. It cannot. The employee is the beneficial owner of the account through a trustee designated by the IRS as being authorized to serve in that capacity. The account registration will read like this: "ABC Trust Company Trustee for the Benefit of John Doe."

Second, Karl had a good track record. He had worked and been the sole provider for 31 years. He had taken good care of his family. June had never gone without a meal nor had she ever slept without a roof over her head. Even though he has a tendency to procrastinate, Karl assured June and me in our meeting that he would not leave his present job until he found another one with adequate income and health benefits, and he was sending out résumés daily to companies in his industry for which his skill package would demand a salary commensurate with the one he would be leaving. He was trying to find a full-time job as an employee with a large company where health benefits would be available with no preexisting condition clause for the group coverage.

Third, assuming Karl found a job with the needed health benefits, June didn't understand the investment risks connected with taking the lump sum. She needed to be educated. But on this particular day, she could not see beyond the urgent concerns she had about their income and health benefits. Any time spent discussing investment returns and risks would be time wasted.

So our main task was to explain to June that the decision to take the buyout or not was not solely up to Karl, to reinforce the fact that Karl had never let her down, and to realistically compare the scenarios from which they could choose.

Thirty minutes into our meeting, Karl remarked, "Your didn't realize this would be a marriage counseling session, did you?" What

Karl and June didn't know was that every financial planning session is a marriage counseling session to the degree that there are unresolved issues in a marriage that carry financial implications.

The issue for this couple was communication. As in many marriages, it is difficult to find time to sit down and discuss emotionally loaded concerns. Often, the financial planning session provides that opportunity. The best financial planners will realize this and be equipped to help work through those issues.

BUILDING RETIREMENT SECURITY: THE NUTS AND BOLTS

If you find yourself at 50 with nothing, the retirement nest egg you will need will be determined by the annual cost of living you will need to maintain. Some people will need $1 million or more. Others will need much less. Work your way through the following sections to determine how close you are to your retirement goal. If you will have a pension but you know it won't be enough to completely support your cost of living, the Retirement Income Calculator at the end of this chapter will allow you to account for the pension amount and tell you how much else you will need.

Starting with Nothing at 50

If you've only just begun to start saving for retirement at 50, you must develop a financial blueprint and follow through with it in a disciplined way. Before you attempt to estimate anything, you must first carefully identify what it costs you to maintain your standard of living.

- Use the household and family expense worksheet in Appendix B to classify each check and credit card expenditure for the past year. Project the changes you might expect in your cost of living for retirement. For example, work-related expenses, such as parking fees, lunches out, uniform cleaning, and 401(k) contributions, will be eliminated at retirement. Other expenses may go up, such as travel and entertainment. Spend some time developing these numbers as they will define your lifestyle at retirement. Once you have the numbers, you are ready to proceed to the next sections.

- Figure out ways to cut your costs and redirect those dollars to retirement savings. You'll have to compromise. You'll probably have to perform your own household chores instead of hiring someone else to do them. That will save you money. *Example:* Mow your own lawn; cook and eat at home instead of eating out; divide up the home cleaning tasks and do them yourselves.

- Analyze your spending and identify "wants" versus "needs." You can do this by studying the household and family expense sheet you completed from Appendix B. Then spend as little as possible on "wants." *Example:* Paying the mortgage or your rent is a need. Most clothes are wants. Buying expensive gifts are wants. Making a gift of homemade goodies or sending cards are needs.

- Invest at least 20 percent of your gross income.

- Set as a goal to earn at least 12 percent per year as an average annual return on your investments.

- Diversify your investments. You can't afford to make a mistake so you must be conservative at this point. Use the services of a good mutual fund family that has a variety of funds from which to select. Make sure you include funds of domestic large, medium-size, and small companies' stocks and bonds. Don't overlook the importance of diversifying worldwide within the family of funds.

- Maximize the amount you can place into your tax-deductible plans at work. *Example:* 401(k) plans are tax deductible; straight mutual fund investments are not.

- Take advantage of tax-deferred investments outside your tax-deductible plan by using variable annuities and variable life insurance products. Every nickel you save in taxes earns you dollars of growth in your retirement portfolio. Variable annuities and variable life insurance products are perfect for the person in his or her fifties who has maxed out their tax-deductible retirement contributions.

- If necessary, postpone full retirement. After completing the Retirement Income Calculator, you may find the amount you need to invest for retirement is too much when you take into account your income and cost of living needs. If that is the case, don't feel bad about readjusting your retirement horizon. You will probably live to 100 anyway; so just plan to work till 70. You will still have 25 or 30 years to enjoy retirement.

Build Retirement Security by Taking These Steps:

1. Carefully identify what it costs you to maintain your standard of living. See Appendix B for a worksheet to help you.

2. Estimate your anticipated cost of living at retirement. Use the same worksheet in Appendix B.

3. Complete the Retirement Income Calculator at the end of this chapter.

4. Take action. Invest 20 to 25 percent of your income in a diversified selection of mutual funds.

5. Choose mutual funds that will net at least 12 percent a year (after the mutual funds' fees). Playing catch-up in your 50s means you will have to seek more aggressive funds. The luxury of indexed funds won't be a good option for you unless you have large amounts to invest.

6. Maximize your tax-deductible investment opportunities.

7. Work like a trojan for the next 15 years. These are your peak earning years. Your dreams can become realities!

So You Want to Be a Millionaire by 65!

If you want to be a millionaire by 65 and you haven't started yet, I've provided a chart in Chapter 11 to show how much you need to invest at different ages and at varied rates of return to reach millionaire status by the year you designate.

Selecting your investment return is critical. You'll notice that greater returns require lower amounts to invest. Remember, however, that the higher returns also require greater risk tolerance.

Also, be aware that index funds will perform almost exactly as the unmanaged index. (Index funds usually charge around .5 percent as an annual fee.) For example, the S&P 500 index will show you the approximate return you would have realized over the years, and any fund that is "indexed" to the S&P will produce those approximate results.

Appendix A contains the average annual returns of the S&P 500 as well as other asset classes dating back to 1926. You'll see that the S&P 500 index has produced a 10.8 percent per year return on average. Some mutual funds do not outperform the index, whereas a much smaller number do.

Unless you have relatively large amounts of money to invest, you'll have to catch up by finding better returns than those the index has provided in the past. (Refer to Chapter 7 to learn how to select mutual funds that can help you catch up faster.)

If you are 50 or 55, take a look at the chart below to see how much you would have to invest to reach $1 million by age 65.

$1 Million by Age 65

Age	Investment Amount/Month	Investment Return
50	$2,392	10%/yr
	1,982	12%/yr
	1,632	14%/yr
55	4,841	10%/yr
	4,304	12%/yr
	3,815	14%/yr

These dollar amounts may seem like a lot of money. And they are. However, let's take a look at what may be possible for you.

If you want to be a millionaire by age 65, you have a lot of catching up to do. That means you will have to invest a larger-than-normal percentage of your income, and you must earn at least a 12 percent return on your money each year. Furthermore, you must be earning between $95,000 and $120,000 a year for this formula to work. Take a look

Annual Income	% Invested	Monthly Investments
$ 95,136	25%	$1,982
$118,920	20%	$1,982

If your income can't meet these levels, you probably don't need $1 million for retirement capital anyway. So you should immediately proceed to the next section to determine exactly what you need to do to adequately cover your costs of living in retirement.

Retirement Income Calculator

SECTION 1		*YOU*	*EXAMPLE*
Line 1:	Fill in your current annual before-tax cost of living:	$_____	$ 50,000
Line 2:	Multiply your figure from line 1 by 75%: This is your estimated *current value* of your before-tax annual retirement cost of living.	$_____	$ 37,500
Line 3:	Fill in the annual rate of inflation you expect between now and the time you retire (3% to 6%)	_____%	3%
Line 4:	Fill in the number of years you expect to continue working before you retire:	_____yrs	15 yrs
Line 5:	Use your figures from lines 3 and 4 to determine in Figure 4.1 your appropriate inflation factor:	_____	1.558
Line 6:	Multiply your figure from line 2 by the inflation factor from line 5: This is your estimated *future value* of your before-tax annual retirement cost of living.	_____	$ 58,425
Line 7:	Divide line 6 by 7% (.07): This is the total amount of retirement capital in future dollars you will need to provide the income in line 6.	$_____	$834,643

Retirement Income Calculator

SECTION 2	*YOU*	*EXAMPLE*
List assets you currently own that are intended to grow until retirement:		

Asset #1: _____	$_____	$150,000
Asset #2: _____	_____	$ 35,000
Asset #3: _____	_____	0
Line 1: Total:	_____	$185,000

Line 2: Estimate the annual rate of return you expect to get from your retirement capital between now and the time that you retire: _____%   10%

Line 3: Fill in the number of years you expect to continue working before you retire: _____yrs   15 yrs

Line 4: Use your figures from lines 2 and 3 to determine in Figure 4.1 your appropriate retirement capital appreciation factor: _____   4.177

Line 5: Multiply your figure from line 1 by the appreciation factor from line 4: $_____ $772,745
This is the *future value* of your current retirement capital account.

Line 6: Subtract line 5 of Section 2 from line 7 of Section 1. If the balance is zero or negative, stop here— congratulations! You have an adequate amount saved for your retirement income needs. If the balance is positive, note the amount: $_____ $61,898

Line 7: Divide line 6 by $1,000,000: _____   .0619

Line 8: Using the figures from lines 2 and 3 in Section 2, determine in Figure 4.2 below the unadjusted monthly investment amount needed to satisfy your retirement income goal: $___/mo $2,413/month

Line 9: Multiply line 7 by line 8: $___/mo $149/month

FIGURE 4.1 The Compound Value of One Dollar

This table provides you with what one dollar will be worth if it earns the interest rates shown on the top line for the varied number of years shown in the first column on the left. Using this table will give you a shortcut in determining what retirement capital you will have if it's invested at the selected rate of return for the number of years you will require.

Period	3%	4%	5%	6%	7%	8%	10%	12%	14%
1	1.030	1.040	1.050	1.060	1.070	1.080	1.100	1.120	1.140
2	1.061	1.082	1.102	1.124	1.145	1.166	1.210	1.254	1.300
3	1.093	1.125	1.158	1.191	1.225	1.260	1.331	1.405	1.482
4	1.126	1.170	1.216	1.262	1.311	1.360	1.464	1.574	1.689
5	1.159	1.217	1.276	1.338	1.403	1.469	1.611	1.762	1.925
6	1.194	1.265	1.340	1.419	1.501	1.587	1.772	1.974	2.195
7	1.230	1.316	1.407	1.504	1.606	1.714	1.949	2.211	2.502
8	1.267	1.369	1.477	1.594	1.718	1.851	2.144	2.476	2.853
9	1.305	1.423	1.551	1.689	1.838	1.999	2.358	2.773	3.252
10	1.344	1.480	1.629	1.791	1.967	2.159	2.594	3.106	3.707
11	1.384	1.539	1.710	1.898	2.105	2.332	2.853	3.479	4.226
12	1.426	1.601	1.796	2.012	2.252	2.518	3.138	3.896	4.818
13	1.469	1.665	1.886	2.133	2.410	2.720	3.452	4.363	5.492
14	1.513	1.732	1.980	2.261	2.579	2.937	3.797	4.887	6.261
15	1.558	1.801	2.079	2.397	2.759	3.172	4.177	5.474	7.138
16	1.605	1.873	2.183	2.540	2.952	3.426	4.595	6.130	8.137
17	1.653	1.948	2.292	2.693	3.159	3.700	5.054	6.866	9.276
18	1.702	2.026	2.407	2.854	3.380	3.996	5.560	7.690	10.575
19	1.754	2.107	2.527	3.026	3.617	4.316	6.116	8.613	12.056
20	1.806	2.191	2.653	3.207	3.870	4.661	6.727	9.646	13.743
25	2.094	2.666	3.386	4.292	5.427	6.848	10.835	17.000	26.462
30	2.427	3.243	4.322	5.743	7.612	10.063	17.449	29.960	50.950

FIGURE 4.2   Monthly Investment Needed to Have
$1 Million at Retirement

Working Years Remaining	Expected Rate of Return			
	8%	10%	12%	14%
5	$13,610	$12,914	$12,244	$11,602
6	$10,867	$10,193	$ 9,550	$ 8,939
7	$ 8,920	$ 8,268	$ 7,653	$ 7,073
8	$ 7,470	$ 6,841	$ 6,253	$ 5,705
9	$ 6,352	$ 5,745	$ 5,184	$ 4,667
10	$ 5,466	$ 4,882	$ 4,347	$ 3,860
11	$ 4,749	$ 4,187	$ 3,678	$ 3,220
12	$ 4,158	$ 3,617	$ 3,134	$ 2,705
13	$ 3,664	$ 3,145	$ 2,687	$ 2,284
14	$ 3,247	$ 2,749	$ 2,314	$ 1,938
15	$ 2,890	$ 2,413	$ 2,002	$ 1,651
16	$ 2,583	$ 2,126	$ 1,737	$ 1,410
17	$ 2,316	$ 1,879	$ 1,512	$ 1,208
18	$ 2,083	$ 1,665	$ 1,320	$ 1,037
19	$ 1,878	$ 1,479	$ 1,154	$ 892
20	$ 1,698	$ 1,317	$ 1,011	$ 769
25	$ 1,051	$ 754	$ 532	$ 371
30	$ 671	$ 442	$ 286	$ 182

Answering Your Financial
Wake-Up Call at 65:
Is It Too Late?

"Necessity makes even the timid brave."

—*Sallust*

*T*he oldest boomers, now in their late 40s and early 50s, have little more than ten years left before they reach 65, the traditional age of retirement. For those who have not yet begun to save for the golden years, time is running out. Once we reach our mid-60s, our capacity to earn top dollars and the level of energy required to do so typically decrease. By then we are more interested in working at a slower pace instead of the hectic dawn-to-dusk pace we kept in our earlier years.

If you reach 65 without having secured your financial future, it is too late. You will have no choice but to continue to work and in all likelihood to lower your standard of living. The good news for boomers is that if they're reading this book, they aren't yet 65 and still have time. The good news for readers who are already 65 is that they are probably in good health and will want to work past age 65.

After all, retirement and age are all relative. Some want to quit at 55, others at 65, and others still at 75!

But let's talk about the 65-year-old who has inadequate retirement assets but wants to retire—or at least semiretire!

THE COLD HARD REALITY—NO PLACE TO HIDE

Stan Torgerson, former business editor of the *Meridian Star* in my hometown of Meridian, Mississippi, likens the plight of the 65-year-old without retirement assets to his predicament when his kidney stones reached the point of no return. "Years ago I developed kidney stones," he writes. "Anyone who has ever had them understands. They produce some of the most intense pain known to man." He continues:

> I was broadcasting professional baseball at the time and was scheduled to leave for spring training in a very few days. I had had previous attacks, but this night I had a roll-on-the-living-room-floor-and-wish-to-die attack. The doctor put the fire out with medication, then informed me I needed an operation and the sooner the better. "Doctor," I said, "I'm going to Florida, and I'll have it done after I get back."
>
> The look on his face was unmistakable. "Young man," he said, "this time there is no place to hide."

If you are 65 with no retirement assets, there's no place for you to hide. What to do? In their book, *Age Wave,* Ken Dychtwald and Joe Fowler characterize the financial styles of boomers' grandparents, boomers' parents, and boomers themselves in the following way. The point of view of grandparents of boomers, deeply influenced by the depression of the 1930s, is: "Save, save, save. Something terrible could happen, and you must be prepared for that rainy day." The attitude of parents of boomers, influenced in part by the depression and in part by the prosperity that followed World War II, is: "Save some, spend some." The danger faced by boomers, influenced by post-World War II prosperity, in planning for retirement is captured by this attitude: "If you have no money in the bank, but you have at least two credit cards that aren't over the limit, you're doing fine." Well, at age 65 you won't be!

In all probability, though, some of you for a variety of reasons will reach age 65 without having broken your old spending habits and without having made financial preparations for retirement. Let's be optimistic and presume this is a cautionary chapter for you. I don't have many clients who have reached age 65 with no retirement funds and can only surmise those people don't seek financial planners because they don't have money to invest. For those few who do see me, two major areas need tackling. Their cost of living had to be examined to find ways to drastically cut expenses, and income sources had to be evaluated to determine how to create enough money to cover reduced living costs.

Cost-of-Living Reductions

To survive by earning some money and supplementing it with Social Security benefits, you have to evaluate several elements of your cost of living.

The first of those elements is taxes. If taxes can be reduced, the outflow of money can be reduced. One way to reduce taxes is to move to a state with lower or no state income taxes. A number of states in warmer climates offer that benefit. Figure 5.1 shows income tax rates of various states. Seriously consider moving to save state taxes.

Meridian business writer Torgerson adds: "Drive that old car one more year and then drive it another and another. You'll save serious money in less costly license plates and lower insurance rates."

The second area where reductions can be made is housing. If at all possible, it's best to eliminate house payments. Some people sell their homes and use the equity to pay cash for a smaller home, which in some cases is a condominium. Others explore updated versions of old housing ideas such as manufactured homes. The National Commission on Manufactured Housing reports that manufactured housing provides a home-ownership option for some 15.4 million persons who may not be able to afford other housing. So a move into a manufactured home in a state with little or no state income taxes is not out of the question.

The American Association of Retired Persons (AARP) produced a detailed report, dated April 22, 1998, covering the positives and negatives of manufactured housing for seniors, and also reported a story about Lucy Coleman.

FIGURE 5.1   State Income Tax Rates

	%		%
Alabama	5.00	Montana	11.00
Alaska	0.00	Nebraska	6.99
Arizona	5.60	Nevada	0.00
Arkansas	7.00	New Hampshire	5.00
California	11.00	New Jersey	6.58
Colorado	5.00	New Mexico	8.50
Connecticut	4.50	New York	7.50
Delaware	7.70	North Carolina	7.75
District of Columbia	9.50	North Dakota	12.00
Florida	0.00	Ohio	7.50
Georgia	6.00	Oklahoma	7.00
Hawaii	10.00	Oregon	9.00
Idaho	8.20	Pennsylvania	2.80
Illinois	3.00	Rhode Island	9.90
Indiana	3.40	South Carolina	7.00
Iowa	9.98	South Dakota	0.00
Kansas	6.45	Tennessee	6.00
Kentucky	6.00	Texas	0.00
Louisiana	6.00	Utah	7.20
Maine	8.50	Vermont	9.00
Maryland	5.00	Virginia	5.75
Massachusetts	12.00	Washington	0.00
Michigan	4.40	West Virginia	6.50
Minnesota	8.50	Wisconsin	6.93
Mississippi	5.00	Wyoming	0.00
Missouri	6.00		

Source: Research Institute of America—All States Tax Guide, 1996.
(Rates listed above represent the highest marginal income tax rate for each state.)

CASE IN POINT

A Senior in a Low-Cost Manufactured Home
(Lucy Coleman)

*T*he AARP's report is as follows:

Almost two years ago Lucy Coleman of Ocala, Florida, traded her conventional two-story house for a manufactured home (many consumers call them mobile homes). Why did she do it? As Coleman puts it, her new home is "affordable, compact and convenient" and she plans to stay there "forever."

Coleman's new home is a far cry from what used to be called a trailer. She bought a finished, 1,200-square-foot, two-bedroom, two-bath home for less than $40,000. That's about $100,000 less than the average price of a new site-built or conventional house. Coleman paid for the manufactured home with the proceeds from the sale of her old house. She banked the difference.

Her new home is installed in a mobile home park with a swimming pool and tennis courts. The park is close to shopping and medical facilities. Although she owns her home, Coleman pays a little over $200 a month in rent for a lot. She pays separately for utilities.

As an older woman, Coleman's certainly not alone in choosing a mobile home. Across the country, more than two million older adults live in manufactured housing. Most live in Sun Belt states like Florida, California, Texas, North Carolina, and Georgia. Affordability seems to be the chief reason older buyers select manufactured housing. Over half of all older mobile home owners have incomes below $20,000 a year.

According to the magazine *American Demographics,* the size and quality of mobile homes has improved and the homes remain affordable. Over half (57 percent) of both younger and older mobile home owners say they plan to remain right where they are.

The number of older owners is also increasing. Four out of every ten new mobile homes are purchased by people over age 50.

Some people aged 65 and older who don't own a home look for housing for seniors that is government assisted. Especially in outlying suburbs and smaller communities, government-assisted programs target senior housing and provide quality, affordable apartment living. The apartment units are the same types as those mentioned in Chapter 6 where I discuss investment options that provide tax credits for the investor. My client, Bette, a younger boomer, actually invested in an affordable housing program and is receiving tax credits for ten years; her 73-year-old aunt lives there.

After considering ways to reduce your state income taxes and housing costs, tackle other elements of your living costs. Editor Torgerson offers the following suggestions:

The five most sensible words: Honey, let's eat at home!   You don't really need to eat out at today's restaurant prices. Travel is not something you can afford. Accept the fact that casinos are in business to make their operators rich, not the customers. Slot machines are not a recreation you can afford.

If you smoke, give up the habit. Both your health and your wallet benefit. One less beer a day won't really bother you but it will save a buck or more. That's $30 per month—good money.

Be sensitive to household expenses. Why leave a television set running in the bedroom when you're in the den? Turn lights off in rooms you are not occupying.

Don't try to buy the affection of your grandchildren with expensive Christmas or birthday gifts. If your kids have trained their children properly, they'll realize times are hard for grandma and grandpa. They won't expect more than you can afford.

Remember debt is the most serious enemy any retiree, or near retiree, can have. Debt and keeping up with the Joneses have made life miserable for many people in their retirement years.

Does selling your house make sense? Sure, if there is enough equity in it to make life better and simpler. Besides, the dollars are tax-free [under the Tax Simplification Act of 1997]. Whatever price you get, less the remaining mortgage, goes straight into your bank account.

Yes, there is an emotional attachment to a house in which you've lived for 25 or 30 years. It isn't, however, as strong as the emotion you feel when your mailbox is filled with bills and there's no realistic way to pay them.

Give serious thought to the number of your friends who have given up house living and become apartment dwellers. You may be surprised. You'll be trading a mortgage payment for a rent check but the money you'll realize from the sale hopefully will earn interest that will defray the cost of an apartment.

Where Retirement Funds Come From

According to the Social Security Administration, people who turn 65 rely on the following sources for retirement money:

Social Security	21%
Personal savings/investments	34
Pensions and retirement plans	19
Part-time work	24
Miscellaneous	2

CREATING INCOME AFTER 65

People who reach their mid-60s without having established an adequate retirement nest egg to provide income have to work, but at what? If they have the opportunity, some work full-time a bit longer as did Roger, who came to me at age 60, hoping to retire at 67.

CASE IN POINT

Working at Your Usual Profession or Job
(Roger and Marie)

*R*oger and his wife, Marie, have no children but have spent a lot of money during their 40s and 50s, and they still are spending a lot. They had invested some for retirement, but not enough. So Roger, a psychologist, decided to keep working at his same pace for a while longer. He and Marie came to me to see how much longer he will have to work.

After reviewing their cost of living, they decided they didn't want to cut back. They are investing as much as possible now for retirement. They have thought of themselves as conservative investors through the years. But in retrospect they realize they took unnecessary risks through the years and have lost a lot of money. From time to time, Roger would take unnecessary risk by investing without caution on the advice of his stockbroker. All in all, those flyers haven't worked out, and the couple are now ready to be more prudent with their investment decisions.

Here's what an analysis of their retirement income looks like in ten years when Roger is 70.

Retirement Income Analysis

Income Needed

Annual after-tax budget if retired today	$ 84,700
Future annual after-tax budget if retired in 10 years	
(Future dollars calculated for 3% inflation)	$ 113,800
Taxes (estimated at a 26% average)	29,588
Total Annual Retirement Income Needed:	**$ 143,388**

Income Sources

Invested Assets	*Current Value*	*Future Value*
Profit-sharing plan	$263,000	
	(10 years @ 12%)	$ 816,838
Future PSP contributions	$10,000/year	
	(10 years @ 12%)	196,546
Real estate interest	80,000	201,000*
Total income account		$1,214,384
Percent of income to withdraw		× 8%
Investment income		$ 97,151
Roger's Social Security income		26,400
Total Annual Income Available		**$ 123,551**
Shortfall		**$ 19,837**

*Estimated sales price in ten years.

They will have a $19,837 annual income shortfall. Because they don't want to cut their cost of living, Roger will have to work part-time after age 70 and won't be able to consider quitting at 67. If it were possible to achieve 15 percent average annual return between now and ten years from now, Roger would be able to quit work completely at age 70. The other option would be to reconsider reducing their cost of living.

Roger has decided "flyers" aren't for him, but he needs to take some moderately aggressive risk. Mutual funds with a slightly higher risk could provide the return they need. With these funds, however, Roger and Marie will have to be prepared to ride out more significant downturns than they would have otherwise. By using mutual funds instead of individual stocks, they will be theoretically incurring less risk.

Finding Part-Time Work—Trying Something New

Most people who must continue to work well into their 60s or 70s try to find jobs that are less stressful than full-time work, perhaps part-time work in fields for which they are qualified. Some who are good with numbers find a small business or doctor's office that needs a part-time bookkeeper. A side benefit for them is access to medical or dental care at greatly reduced costs. Some who like socializing and chatting with people follow my Aunt Becky's example. She became a hostess at a restaurant and enjoyed free meals. Some people who particularly like being with children get a job with a day care center or keep a few children in their home.

Such jobs don't have to be stressful. Evaluate your competencies and find a part-time job that capitalizes on your strengths. Think about the things you enjoy and find work that supports your hobbies. Two of my clients who love golf are now working at a country club. One is keeping greens and the other is a starter. They both enjoy the fringe benefit of free golf when they aren't working.

If you're handy, explore a job as a maintenance manager of an apartment complex or manager of the complex and live there for free. If you like caring for the elderly, work for an assisted-living community or nursing home as a receptionist, activities director, or in the food service area; and again live there at reduced rates or even for free.

If you like to travel, work for a travel agency and get free trips. If you like people, perhaps you can work for a department or clothing store and get reduced prices. A writer could get a job with the daily newspaper and write articles from home. One of my clients, Annie, edits books from her home. My friend William likes the symphony, so he volunteers to usher and attends all concerts free. These are all quality-of-life issues structured at reasonable or no cost so seniors can enjoy life and not pay a fortune for it. These are the years to find work that is fun but carries extra benefits.

Available Help

Remember to inquire about senior discounts available at restaurants, movies, and motels, and for train and airline tickets.

Not all of the Social Security income received by those over 65 is taxable. The amount taxed is the lesser of one-half of the annual Social Security benefits received or one-half of the excess of the taxpayer's provisional income over a specified base amount. However, for those at higher income levels, up to 85 percent of the benefits may be taxable. Provisional income is equal to adjusted gross income plus tax-exempt interest plus one-half of Social Security benefits. The base amount is $32,000 for married taxpayers filing jointly, $0 for married taxpayers filing separately, and $25,000 for any other filing status. Up to 85 percent of Social Security benefits are taxable for those who are married and filing jointly with a provisional income in excess of $44,000. Married taxpayers filing separately with a provisional income in excess of $0 and all other taxpayers in excess of $34,000 are affected by the 85 percent inclusion. Not all Social Security income is taxable, but computing the taxes on the part that is taxable is not easy. It is advisable to get assistance with your tax returns for just that reason.

Also, those over 65 receive an extra exemption that reduces taxable income. Nearly all those over 65 are covered by Medicare, and there are programs for subsidized housing, food stamps, and energy assistance that benefit the elderly.

When you turn 65 and you have no retirement assets, with only Social Security income on which to rely, you have a set of problems more difficult to solve than midlife crises and the youthful questions of the future. The time element makes it so. Tackle your financial problems with zeal.

Be creative. There are no easy answers to difficult problems but you *can* find answers. Torgerson has written:

> Remember, the secret of working your way out of a financial predicament is to think. Despair or self-pity won't solve your problems—only make them worse.
>
> Looking back with a "How could I have been so foolish attitude" will do nothing to help.
>
> Look ahead and use the wisdom you hopefully picked up in a lifetime of seeking answers for your employer, your children, or your friends. This time use it for yourself. Remember Colonel Sanders invented Kentucky Fried Chicken when he was in his late sixties. Many others have salvaged or created careers in what were supposed to be their retirement years.
>
> Just make up your mind that for you, the fat lady hasn't sung yet!

Suggestions for People 65 and Over Who Have No Retirement Income Or Reasons for Boomers to Plan for Retirement Now

- *Look for ways to cut down on taxes.* One way is to move to a state with low or no state income taxes.

- *Make housing adjustments.* These may include selling a large home and using the equity to pay cash for a smaller home. Eliminate mortgage payments if at all possible.

- *Eliminate or cut down on restaurant meals.*

- *Eliminate or cut down on travel.*

- *Cut everyday household expenses such as utilities and cable channels.*

- *Avoid debt.*

- *Supplement your income by finding a job that is less stressful than full-time work.*

- *Use senior discounts at restaurants, movies, and motels, and for trains and airlines.*

The Basics of Investing for Retirement

Banks, Insurance Companies, and Brokerage Firms

Smor-gas-bord /n: a luncheon or supper buffet offering a variety of foods and dishes (as hors d'oeuvres, hot and cold meats, smoked and pickled fish, cheeses, salads, and relishes)

Caf-e-te-ria /n: a restaurant in which the customers serve themselves or are served at a counter and take the food to tables to eat

—Webster's New Collegiate Dictionary

I've always found it a bit overwhelming to approach a cafeteria line or a smorgasbord laden with mounds of appetizing food set out for me to enjoy. Because there are so many dishes, I know I will be able to select only some of them and will have to balance my selections. There's no way I can load my plate with only the fabulous-looking desserts. No, I will forgo a dessert feast in favor of a balanced meal; some vegetables, some meat or a protein substitute, perhaps some bread, probably some fruit, and maybe a single dessert. Selecting investments is somewhat analogous to the cafeteria or smorgasbord experience. Choices—intelligent choices—must be made by boomers who take charge of their retirement planning, and they must be knowledgeable enough to balance choices.

Like the cafeteria line, several choices are available in the investment line. Let's examine the line, proceeding from the most conservative to the most aggressive. We'll stop first at the bank, then on to the insurance company, and finish at the brokerage firm, where we find bonds, stocks, real estate, options, commodities, and futures.

Although stressed-out boomers may not want to learn all there is to know about investment alternatives, they should at least know a succinct number of critical facts in order to ask the right questions. This chapter is devoted to a short overview of the array of investment choices.

BANKS

A bank, with several options for placing investment dollars, is our first stop on the cafeteria line of investments.

We can choose to open a checking account. Some checking accounts carry interest and others don't. These accounts are primarily useful for paying household bills and should not be used for retirement investments.

Second, we can choose to open a money market account for our savings or rainy-day money. Money market accounts generally pay interest rates that are higher than interest rates offered with checking accounts. They also usually restrict the number of checks you can write monthly and sometimes require higher minimum balances.

Third, we can choose to open a passbook savings account. Passbook savings accounts typically don't offer check-writing privileges and they usually don't pay interest rates as high as money market accounts.

With all of the options above, you have immediate access to your money with no penalty. The bank offers a fourth investment vehicle, which, like the other three options, has no purchase costs. This fourth option is a certificate of deposit (CD), which you can purchase for a pre-scribed length of time (called its maturity date) to earn a specific interest rate for that term. Although no fee is assessed to purchase a CD, you will be charged a penalty if you cash it in before it has matured.

These four vehicles are the only investments offered at the bank that are both owned and controlled by the bank. For these investment options, the bank buys insurance from the Federal Deposit Insurance Corporation (FDIC) and, therefore, each account is insured against loss up to $100,000.

Planning for bank investments in your portfolio.   Bank investments should be used for your emergency cash reserves and working capital. Investments in banks that are FDIC insured are not suitable for retirement investments from which you expect growth. It has been said that a CD is, in the eyes of a retirement investor, really a "certificate of disappointment."

> *"Last night I read a book that brought tears to my eyes—it was my bank book."*
>
> —*Anonymous, from* Wall Street Wit and Wisdom

Decide how much cash you would need if you lost your job based on how long you think it would take you to replace your job. For some of you, one month is enough to replace your current job; for others, six months or more may be necessary. In general, it takes one month of job searching for each $10,000 of salary expected.

Some mistakenly think mutual fund investments can serve as sources of ready cash. If your paycheck is the only source of family income, don't place yourself in the precarious position of having to cash out your funds if the market takes a sudden downturn just when you need the money. Keep emergency money in your savings or money market accounts.

Other Investments Offered by Banks

> *"CDs and Treasury bills are not investments—just places to park your money while you decide where to invest."*
>
> —*Anonymous, from* Wall Street Wit and Wisdom

With the recent changes in banking laws, a variety of investments that are neither owned nor controlled by banks can now be offered to bank customers. To offer those investments, banks have to either own a brokerage firm or in some way form a partnership or alliance with a brokerage firm. Through that relationship, banks can offer all the investments discussed at each succeeding stop on the cafeteria line of investments.

INSURANCE COMPANIES

Insurance companies offer investments in connection with their products. Insurance products we are most familiar with are the four classifications of life insurance:

1. Term life
2. Whole life
3. Universal life
4. Variable universal life

Insurance products usually are not thought of as investments, but insurance companies offer annuities as investment alternatives, and some believe life insurance can be structured to achieve investment status.

The most recognizable investment options offered by insurance companies are annuities, of which there are two types: fixed annuities and variable annuities.

Fixed Annuities

To easily understand a fixed annuity, think of it as a CD that is issued, not by a bank, but by an insurance company. The similarity is that both investment alternatives carry a fixed interest rate guaranteed for a fixed period of time. In addition, both are insured: a bank CD is insured by the FDIC and a fixed annuity by the insurance company. There, however, the similarity ends.

The differences between a CD and a fixed annuity are related to the amount of the interest, the taxation of the interest, and the penalty period for withdrawal. A fixed annuity usually pays a bit higher interest than a CD. In addition, if you own a CD, you will have to pay taxes on the interest every year even if you reinvest the interest. If you own a fixed annuity, taxes are deferred on the reinvested interest.

If you own a CD, you will be assessed a penalty if you cash it in before it has matured. With a fixed annuity you will be assessed a penalty if you cash it in before a long period of time—perhaps as many as 7 to 12 years. The penalty is stiff because it is applied to the principal as well as the interest earned. It is not uncommon to see penalties begin in the first year at 7 percent but decline to 0 percent if you hold the annuity for 7 or more years.

One final restriction is associated with a fixed annuity but does not apply to CDs. If you withdraw the interest from the annuity before you're 59½, the IRS will penalize you 10 percent on the amount withdrawn. Annuities are generally viewed by the IRS as retirement vehicles: thus, the 10 percent penalty for early withdrawal.

Variable Annuities

An investment comparable to a variable annuity is a mutual fund. Visualize an umbrella called an insurance company under which you place your mutual funds. As an investor in mutual funds, you enjoy returns from rising stock or bond markets while suffering the consequences of market downturns. But as with the fixed annuity, under the shelter offered by the umbrella of the insurance company, all reinvested dividends and capital gains from variable annuities are not taxed annually. They are taxed only when they are withdrawn. Be aware also that there are fixed-rate options available under variable annuities.

As with the fixed annuity, if you withdraw the dividends and capital gains before age 59½, you will be assessed not only the taxes but also a 10 percent penalty by the IRS. Therefore, consider all annuities as vehicles for retirement investments if you are under 59½. If you are over 59½, annuities offer a great place to invest for tax-deferred earnings. However, many annuity purchases are restricted to people under age 85.

While it is possible to invest retirement dollars into variable annuities, and they are widely touted by insurance agents and insurance-oriented planners as good IRA investment vehicles, it turns out to be an expensive way to invest in mutual fund–type accounts. The annual fees for these managed accounts are usually about double the annual fees for similarly managed mutual funds purchased outside the variable annuity umbrella. Further, because both qualified-plan dollars (IRAs, pension and profit-sharing plans, simplified employee pensions (SEPs), SIMPLE IRAs) and variable annuities are ways to defer taxes, it doesn't seem to make sense to place already tax-deferred dollars into a vehicle (such as a variable annuity) designed to provide tax-deferred growth but where annual fees are greater. The tax-deferred redundancy costs you in the long run.

Life Insurance as an Investment

A major question is whether to buy a type of life insurance that allows growth of your cash value or to buy term life insurance and invest the difference you thereby save. The permanent versus temporary insurance argument has been around for many years. Here's the bottom line.

Term life insurance.   Term insurance is temporary insurance because you are insured for a fixed, prespecified time. As long as you live, you don't get any money back. The premiums go up every year because you are older—and therefore at greater risk of dying. You buy a flat amount of insurance, and the premium is according to your age and health for the amount of insurance you want. The younger you are, the lower the premium. This is the lowest-cost insurance available for young people, but no cash value builds up. When you die, your beneficiaries receive the death benefit tax-free.

Whole life insurance.   This is called permanent insurance because it is with you for life. You buy it at a flat premium amount greater than the true cost of term insurance at your age. While you are young, you are overpaying for the insurance. As you age the true cost catches up to what you are paying each year. The extra money you pay in the early years stays with the insurance company, and they invest it with all their assets. Until the true cost of insurance for your age equals what you are paying, the extra cash buildup is called cash value. The insurance company pays you interest at a low rate on that cash value. It is your money in a "holding account" until the cost of your insurance exceeds what you are paying. The company then dips into the cash value account and pays the difference, thus guaranteeing you a death benefit for your whole life. One final feature: you can borrow your cash value from the policy (usually at very low rates) tax-free, although you must never borrow more than about 85 to 90 percent of the cash available in your cash value account. Whole life, then, is a package that provides you insurance for your whole life if you pay premiums for your whole life.

Universal life.   This is the contract through which you ask the insurance company to let your premium dollars participate in interest rate fluctuations. In return, the company may ask you to pay premiums for a longer period of time to make up for lower interest rates than were originally expected.

Universal life insurance is exactly like whole life except that

- your cash value earns interest consistent with money market rates;
- when interest rates go down, you may have to pay a higher premium;
- you can lower the death benefit and thus lower your premium; and
- you could end up with no death benefit if your premiums are inadequate to pay for the term insurance as you age.

Variable universal life.   This is the contract through which you elect to have your premium dollars invested in the stock or bond markets through mutual fund agreements with the insurance company. You participate in both up and down markets and your premium is adjusted accordingly.

Variable universal life is exactly like universal life except that

- your cash value can be directed by you into a variety of different investment options such as mutual funds or money market accounts;
- your cash value is held for you in a separate account within the insurance company;
- because over time potential stock market returns have historically been somewhat greater than interest rates, you could find enough cash in your policy in your 60s to borrow for supplemental income during retirement; and
- variable life insurance is the hottest product on the market today, with many using it to buy life insurance in addition to building up cash tax-free for supplemental retirement income.

Planning for insurance company investments in your portfolio.   Some of the investment options offered by insurance companies are alternatives for retirement investing worth considering. If you have maximized your contributions to a 401(k), pension, profit-sharing, or other tax-deferred investment plan and you still want tax-deferred growth from your investment dollars, consider an alternative offered by insurance companies. See Figure 6.1 to help you decide what type of insurance policy would be an appropriate retirement vehicle for you.

With a variable life policy, not only do you get a death benefit, but you get an added feature. You can take money out of your policy at any time without taxation. The longer you wait to withdraw the money, potentially the more you can withdraw. When you do take the money out, you will be sent the principal you invested first, which is called "return of capital." Next, you will be allowed to borrow against your cash value (which would have been invested in mutual funds and, it is hoped, grown considerably). If you leave the money to grow until you retire, presumably at age 65, it will have grown to the greatest amount and will provide you tax-free income for your retirement years. It is tax-free because you are borrowing against the policy. A word of caution: If you take money out of the policy in the first ten years, you will pay a penalty and

FIGURE 6.1   Life Insurance Rated as a Vehicle for Retirement Planning

	Premiums	*Cash Accumulation*	*Rating as Retirement-Planning Vehicle*
Term	Lowest	None	Poor
Whole	Fixed and usually highest	Depends on insurance company management of assets	Fair
Universal	Can fluctuate	Depends on interest rates	Modest
Variable universal life	Can fluctuate	Depends on returns and your selection of investments	Best

could actually lose money. If you ever let a variable life policy lapse, you will have to pay taxes on all you have borrowed over the amount you invested in the policy.

BROKERAGE OR FINANCIAL PLANNING FIRM

The next stop on the cafeteria line of investments is the brokerage or financial planning firm, where you'll find a variety of investment alternatives, including all the ones available through banks or insurance companies. The investments most commonly associated with brokerage firms are the ones addressed below: bonds, stocks, mutual funds, real estate investment trusts and limited partnerships, options, futures, and precious metals.

Bonds

Except for investments offered by banks and insurance companies, bonds are the most conservative. (See Figure 6.2.) A bond is a piece of paper indicating that the bondholder has lent money to the company or

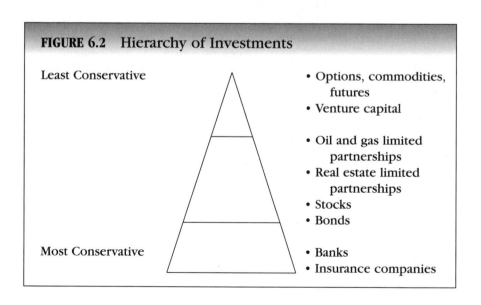

FIGURE 6.2 Hierarchy of Investments

Least Conservative

- Options, commodities, futures
- Venture capital

- Oil and gas limited partnerships
- Real estate limited partnerships
- Stocks
- Bonds

Most Conservative

- Banks
- Insurance companies

government issuing the bond. In return for the loan, the issuer will pay interest on the bond every six months. There are corporate and government bonds from which to choose; and some bonds issued by governments pay tax-free interest.

Bonds are rated by Standard and Poor's for their financial stability. The highest-rated bonds carry AAA ratings. Generally, the more As, the safer the bond. If the bond is rated B or C, you can surmise its financial stability is weaker than if it were rated A.

If bond issuers are financially unstable, they generally have to offer bond purchasers a higher interest rate to successfully sell their bonds. These bonds are called high-yield or high-income bonds and are loosely referred to as junk bonds. A bond is considered to be junk if the company or government that issued it has a likelihood of going out of business, in which case those who bought the bond lose not only their interest but also their principal.

Ruby came to see me for financial advice. She told me she had invested $15,000 in Eastern Airline bonds in the declining years of Eastern. While it was in business, she earned 20 percent interest on the bonds. However, when it went out of business, she lost the interest Eastern still owed her as well as her original $15,000 investment. She was now searching for investments that would help her avoid that kind of loss again.

Traditionally, we think of bonds as being safe, which translates in our minds as "guaranteed" or "will not ever be less than what I paid for it." However, bonds and interest rates sit on opposite ends of a seesaw. When the interest rate goes up, the value of the bond goes down, and the reverse is true. So, for example, if you buy a bond when interest rates are 4 percent and then interest rates rise, you may want to sell your bond to earn the higher interest rates in the market. If you do sell your bond, you will receive less than you paid for it. Notice on the Ibbotson chart in Appendix A how interest rate fluctuations shown in the Treasuries bar chart have caused decreases in the corporate and government bond bar charts. As you study those charts and realize that over time your average annual rate of return would have been around 5 percent while, you were taking some risk, it may prompt you to consider investing in the stock market as evidenced by the performances shown in the bar charts of the S&P 500.

"Stocks have outperformed bonds in each of the nine decades of this century except one—the 1930s."

—*Anonymous, from* Wall Street Wit and Wisdom

Planning for bonds in your portfolio.   Bonds are appropriate for people who do not expect to live at least 15 more years and aren't interested in leaving any assets for the next generation. This is because the interest and principal are fixed and both may have to be spent in a person's later years when inflation has pushed up the cost of living. They are also appropriate for very conservative investors who have enough money to enjoy the luxury of taking little or no risk except that of spending their principal if they should need it in the future when inflation has eroded the purchasing power of their fixed income.

In their book *Die Broke,* Stephen M. Pollan and Mark Levine warn against comparing the returns from stocks to the returns from bonds, saying it's like comparing apples and oranges. "Bonds will never offer the growth rates of the best-performing stocks," they say. "But stocks will never offer the security and certainty of the best-performing bonds. Of course, nothing is for certain. Bonds can fall in value if interest rates rise."

Stocks

One step farther along on the cafeteria line of investments are conservative stocks—those bought under book value or stocks that historically pay a solid dividend.

It doesn't happen often these days, but sometimes I'm asked, "What exactly is a stock?" To own a piece of a company is to own a stock. While we say "we own a stock," to be technically correct we really should say we own a share or a number of shares of a stock. A share of stock is evidenced by a certificate that has been issued by a company in exchange for a dollar value representing the purchase price of the share or shares of the company's stock. We pay, for example, $60 a share for a stock and we purchase 100 shares. Our cost would be $6,000 for the 100 shares.

How do you buy shares of a stock? You must go to a broker who has access to someone on the floor of the appropriate stock exchange. Brokers charge commissions to purchase your stock. They are employed by a variety of different companies, from large brokerage houses to buying services on the Internet.

To purchase shares through one of the large brokerage houses (called full-service brokers) who advertise on television, we would have to pay a commission in the range of 2 to 5 percent. To purchase the same 100 shares from a discount broker, perhaps at a bank, we would have to pay a commission in the range of 1 to 2 percent. Through the Internet or a few discount brokerage houses, the commission could be as low as a flat fee of $6 to $35. The commission or fee you are willing to pay is determined by how much advice you need. If you are truly a "do-it-yourself" trader, your fees could be quite low. If you need help from a professional, however, you will pay commissions.

The commission is charged when you buy the stock and when you sell it. You make money when you buy a stock at $60 a share and you sell it at $75 a share. Take a look at the following example:

Buy 100 shares at $60 a share	$6,000
Add commission of 4%	× .04
	$240
Total Cost of Trade	$6,240
Sell 100 shares (two years later) at $75 a share	$7,500
Deduct commission of 4%	× .04
	($300)
Total Cost of Trade	$7,200
Your Net Profit	$ 960

To compute your rate of return, divide your profit by the original cost to get your *total* rate of return from the date you purchased the stock until the date you sold it: $960 divided by $6,240 = 15.39 percent total return. To determine your annualized rate of return, divide the total percent return by the total number of years you have held the stock. For example, .1539 divided by 2 years = .07695, or about 7.7 percent annualized rate of return.

Investors often make the mistake of computing their return by ignoring the commissions. If you had made that mistake in this example, you would think you had an annualized rate of return of 12.5 percent instead of the 7.7 percent you really netted.

*"It was the steady investors who kept their heads
when the stock market tanked in October 1987, and
then saw the value of their holding eventually recover
and continue to produce attractive returns."*

—*Burton Malkiel*

Planning for stocks in your portfolio.   If you want your asset growth
to exceed the interest rate percentage you can get in a bank or insurance
company and if you can still sleep at night if your principal goes down
for a time, stocks may have a place in your portfolio.

Stocks are considered investments that over time provide growth.
Therefore, stocks are good for retirement investments. They are usually
grouped into roughly three categories:

1. Growth
2. Growth and income
3. Income

Growth stocks are usually those whose companies keep the dividends
inside the company to "grow" the company. In other words, the company plans to open more plants or stores and needs the money to open
them. Therefore, they don't pay dividends to shareholders. An example
of a growth stock is Home Depot, which pays virtually no dividends. In
general, growth stocks carry the most risk.

Growth and income stocks are usually offered by companies that
enjoy a fairly steady stream of income and need to retain some earnings
to grow the company. Therefore, they pay out some of their cash income
as dividends and keep some for growth. An example is Coca-Cola, which
pays a dividend of about 60¢ per share and produces a yield of about .7
percent (based on a share price of about $81), although its revenues
would support a higher dividend. The company chooses to retain some
potential dividend income to open new markets. Growth and income
stocks are less risky than growth stocks.

Income stocks are usually offered by companies that enjoy a fairly
steady stream of income that they can afford to share with shareholders.
Examples of income stocks are utilities and telecommunications companies, whose subscribers pay monthly bills to provide the steady stream

of income that makes it possible for regular dividends to be paid. An income stock is one where the company pays out a substantial portion of its earnings in dividends to shareholders, keeping less inside the company for growth. It is not uncommon to find a utilities company paying a 5 percent dividend. Income stocks are generally the most conservative.

Typically, utility companies have not been considered high growth as it's unlikely that an individual or a family will double its consumption of gas or electricity. However, telecommunications companies are taking on a different character in today's world. In years past, they were strictly thought of as income companies. Today, however, with the advent of wireless communications and the branching out into the international arena, telecommunications companies are taking on more of a growth focus than in the past.

If you are investing for retirement, you want to focus your stock investments on growth. If you are already retired, you need stocks that offer growth as well as income. Income stocks are typically bought along with some growth stocks to create growth and income for your portfolio.

The January effect:
"January tends to set the tone for the rest of the
market year."

—*Anonymous, from* Wall Street Wit and Wisdom

You may have heard about it, but do you know what the January effect is? Typically, stocks do well in January because it is usually the month during which large companies fund their pension plans for the previous calendar year. It is also the month when many of us are funding IRAs. In

Investing: Longer Is Better

If you examine the patterns over the past 50 years, you can learn some interesting things about stock profits. For instance, the longer you hold on to a stock, the more likely it is you'll make a profit. If you have a stock portfolio for 1 year, you have a 67 percent chance of earning money. Hold the stocks for 5 years and the odds increase to 80 percent. The likelihood of making a profit increases to 96 percent over 10 years, and to 100 percent over 15 years.

addition, January is the month during which those who may have sold stock in December for tax losses buy back into the market. Consequently, these factors plus normal 401(k) monthly fundings generally cause stock prices to go up.

Options, Futures, Precious Metals

"To make a small fortune buying options—start out with a large fortune."

—Wall Street Wit and Wisdom

Options and futures contracts exist for many assets, including stocks, bonds, cotton, sugar, cattle, and most other commodities. A futures contract is an obligation to buy or sell an asset at a predetermined price sometime in the future. Options contracts give the holder the right, but not the obligation, to buy ("call" option) or to sell ("put" option) the asset.

For every dollar made there is a dollar lost and the broker in the middle gets a cut. With those odds, whether entering into futures contracts or buying or selling options, the prospects for a gain are not great.

Planning for options, futures, or precious metals in your portfolio.   A good rule of thumb here is: If you don't understand it, don't do it. Options and futures attract two sorts of investors—the overconfident and the overcautious. Overcautious investors think they can buy put options to protect them from major losses and overconfident investors think they can invest a small amount and reap big rewards by timing it just perfectly. Rarely are either correct. My advice? Stay away!

Real Estate

Every investment asset cycles. Real estate tends to cycle every 10 to 15 years and stocks every 4 to 7 years. Real estate as an investment for the small investor was popular in the early '80s through the use of limited partnerships. There were so many buyers of real estate chasing those investor dollars and the tax benefits were so attractive that real estate values became overpriced. But with the Tax Reform Act of 1986 and the elimination of the lucrative tax benefits, real estate investing came to a halt. Many who had invested through limited partnerships were stuck in those partnerships, and now, some 12 painful years later, investors are still holding partnership interests in which the values are questionable at best and nonexistent at worst.

Today, however, we are seeing a resurgence of real estate as a viable investment option for small investors. By purchasing a rental property, small investors can gain modest tax benefits from the expense write-offs and depreciation as well as realize rental income.

Because boomers are busy people stressed out just by living, they would probably opt out if you added the burden of managing rental property to their agendas. There are, however, other viable alternatives.

Real estate limited partnerships. Just because they are limited partnerships doesn't mean they are automatically bad. Some real estate limited partnership company sponsors actually made it through the past 12 bad years and offer investment opportunities for as little as $5,000. Some limited partnerships allow the investor to be part of a group that buys office buildings and shopping centers for all cash.

In others, the investor can participate in owning real estate (through REITs, discussed below, or limited partnerships) that is leased to popular restaurants, hotels, and a new offering of properties in the health care sector such as assisted living facilities.

The investor usually receives the cash flow from the rental income, sheltered somewhat by the depreciation from the properties. An investor in a partnership arrangement must leave his or her money in until the manager (called the general partner) decides to sell the properties and distribute the cash. The purpose of a real estate investment is to provide diversification and to benefit from the profits being taxed at capital gains rates when the properties are sold.

Leo Wells, of Wells Capital, Inc., likes to quote Wayne Gretsky's response when asked how he became such a great hockey player: "I don't go where the puck is, I go where the puck will be." Wells and many other investment advisers believe now is the time to invest in real estate, because in their opinion the cycle seems to have turned and is now on the upswing.

Tax advantages without managing rental property.   Many boomers are looking for ways to get extra mileage out of their tax dollars. One way is to invest in real estate limited partnerships that purchase affordable housing apartments, projects that carry tax credits. For a one-time investment of $5,000, an investor purchases an interest in an affordable housing tax credit partnership and receives a tax credit of about 13 percent per year for ten years. In other words, the investor receives $6,500 in tax credits for the $5,000 investment in the affordable housing partnership. Investors must continue to own the properties for an additional five years after the tax credits have been received. Investors receive no cash flow—only tax benefits—during the holding period. Then the properties can be sold and, it is hoped, investors can get their money back plus a return if the properties have appreciated.

This investment, like the one mentioned above, is illiquid; that is, investors cannot decide to sell at any given time and get out. Some partnerships can be bought or sold on secondary markets, but the terms are usually not very favorable. As a general custom, investors must wait until the general partner sells on behalf of the entire partnership. The risks of losing your money in a limited partnership include the capability of the general partner to manage properties appropriately and the risk that Congress may alter the tax laws and thereby adversely affect your tax credits. The tax law risk is not likely to be great as Congress has always favored tax benefits for private investors who are willing to fund housing for the less fortunate.

Your biggest risk is investing with an incompetent or dishonest general partner. To protect yourself, carefully review the background and track record provided in the prospectus. If there are any securities violations or bankruptcies, don't invest with that general partner. If a general partner has been in business for more than 20 years with no securities violations, however, your money is probably safe.

Real estate investment trusts (REITs): Making real estate liquid.   If you want to participate in real estate and want the ability to sell and get out at your whim, consider a real estate investment trust (REIT), which is bought and sold in shares in the stock market. This is the only way to buy real estate and keep your investment liquid. In other words, investors can decide on a given day to sell their shares at the market value and be out of the investment. REITs are really like mutual funds of limited partnerships, so there is very good diversification and instant liquidity. One recent development is the availability of new mutual funds specializing in REITs.

There are several mutual funds of REITs available; however, there are only a few funds that are "index REITs." A new mutual fund of REITs has been offered for the first time in 1998 by Wells Real Estate Funds. The fund represents 90 percent of the total U.S. REIT market capitalization. It is marketed as the Wells S&P REIT Index Fund, whose objectives are high dividend yield with capital appreciation. The fund offers its investors tax advantages because REITs are not subject to federal income taxes, assuming they distribute to shareholders at least 95 percent of their taxable income (exclusive of capital gains). Also, distributions paid by REITs often include return of capital. As such, a portion of the dividend is deferred from ordinary income tax. For tax purposes, the shares are treated just like shares of stock.

Vanguard Specialized REIT Index Fund uses the Morgan Stanley REIT Index as their investment index. The screening process differs from the S&P process in several ways. For example, Morgan Stanley represents a lower percentage of the REIT market capitalization, because it doesn't cover the health care sector. S&P also follows stricter guidelines regarding REITs dividend payout and trading history.

Planning for real estate in your portfolio.   If you have maxed out your pretax investment options, perhaps you should look for other ways to receive tax benefits. Investing in real estate provides one option. Rental real estate requires your attention to management, and if your income is between $100,000 and $150,000, you'll lose your tax benefits on a graduated scale.

Sheltered income will be gained from most real estate limited partnerships. Tax credits are the best tax benefits and are gained from affordable housing partnerships. A tax credit is best because it is a direct dollar-for-dollar reduction of your taxes subtracted off the bottom line of your taxes. If you are in the 28 percent or higher tax bracket, it may be appropriate to consider an affordable housing investment. If tax benefits aren't a consideration, consider a REIT for diversification.

CHOOSING SOMEONE TO HELP YOU

Of all the financial advisers available to the average person, certified financial planners are perhaps the best. They are required to be recertified annually by completing a required number of continuing education courses as well as a specific course on the ethics of financial planning. Financial planners understand the pros and cons of most investment opportunities as well as the behavior of money in most every circumstance. Overall, they are honest and your well-being is their overriding concern.

However, just about anyone who is smart enough and willing to go through the required education can become a certified financial planner. Therefore, it is not unusual to find that your financial planner originally began his or her career in a different profession, which will color the planner's opinions about certain areas. If the planner began as an insurance agent, for instance, he or she may give more attention to insurance and less to tax planning or investments. If the planner was an accountant, the first priority might be taxes; if a stock broker, stocks; if a lawyer, estate planning. The very best financial planner is one whose background was unrelated to any of the specific areas addressed by financial planning. That way you are assured the advice will be balanced across all areas—not biased to one.

Qualities of a Good Financial Planner

Here are some specifics to look for in your financial planner. Find a planner who is

- *smart, competent, and well educated.* Look for a person who has invested the time and effort to become licensed as a securities representative, registered investment adviser, certified financial planner, CPA, or attorney. Whatever the license, the person deserves your attention as a recognized professional in the business with meaningful credentials.
- *experienced.* While everyone has to start somewhere, you'll be entrusting decisions about your life savings to this person. A majority of financial planners have been in the business less than four years. Look for someone with at least five years' experience.

- *a good listener* willing to hear your concerns and ideas, not someone who is simply knowledgeable in a number of fields and is pushing a product.
- *not pushy*. Don't be rushed into decisions or be intimidated. Be especially wary of anyone you don't know who wants you to send money after a sales pitch over the phone.
- *practices what they preach*. Why not ask to see the investment portfolio of the financial planner you are considering? If they have done a good job for themselves, they will be proud of it and willing to show you. If they make excuses about why they have failed, remember that it isn't true that the people who have made all the mistakes know how to avoid them. Fact is, they are probably psychologically prone to making mistakes and emotionally hooked on creating problems to solve. As a friend has said, "It's easier to jump on a moving train than it is to start one." Make sure you are jumping on a train moving in a positive direction.
- *trustworthy*. Listen to your feelings. Make sure the person you choose cares about you and the quality of work they do. Financial planning is a people business and your decision should be a people decision. Zig Ziglar has said: "People do not care how much you know until they first know how much you care." The best financial planners practice this in their relationships with the people they serve.

How financial planners are paid.   Financial planners are paid by fees, commissions, or both. Fees range from a one-time flat fee to annual fees charged as a percentage of the amount of money you invest with the planner. Commissions are charged as a percentage of the total amount you spend to buy an investment, as a percentage of the total when you sell out of an investment, or both. Mutual fund commissions are structured as fees when you invest, a fee when you get out of the investment, or a fee (called a 12b-1) charged against your total account value every year.

Don't expect to pay a fee when you meet the planner on the first visit. In fact, as a general rule, if you're charged for the first visit, you can rule that person out. The first meeting should be for getting acquainted and determining if the two of you can work together. Expect to provide complete information for the planner to review at the first meeting. In return, at the end of the meeting a fee or method of compensation should be provided for you along with a complete description of the plan that will be produced for you.

For a list of resources helpful in locating a financial planner, see Appendix E.

Investment Strategies for Playing Retirement Catch-Up

If you're starting late, you'll want to select investments that are aggressive enough to push you along the growth curve as fast as possible. At the same time, you'll need to choose investments that will protect you from catastrophic loss, because you won't have enough time to recoup those losses before you turn 65. Follow our checklist below:

- Become knowledgeable about the selections on the cafeteria line of investments. This will equip you with the appropriate questions to ask and alert you to the potential array of answers. Armed with this knowledge, you can enjoy excellent returns with minimal risk over the long term.

- Use your questions and answers to screen out investments that are not appropriate for you. Use your intuition to help you. If it sounds too good to be true, it probably is—so go another direction.

- Spend time determining your realistic projected retirement date. The longer you have before retirement, the more risk you will be able to take. Some people want to retire in their 50s; others are still happy working at 70, like Walter who retired at 65 as operations manager for a cab company in Memphis. After six months of golf, he got bored and got a job at a resort hotel near his home running the airport shuttle. "Playing golf all the time got just as boring as working all the time," he said. If you are playing catch-up, working part-time after retirement may improve your quality of life and put less stress on your finances than quitting for good.

- Choose someone to help you. Most people spend more time planning a two-week vacation than they do planning their financial future. It is a time-consuming process and you're smart to find a partner to help you.

- After you have done your homework, don't procrastinate—take action. Make investment decisions and follow through with the funding.

The Basics of Investing for Retirement

Mutual Funds

"Don't wait until the time or the market is just right to start investing—start now. The best time to plant an oak tree was 20 years ago—the second best time is now."

—*James Stowers*

*M*utual funds are nothing more than companies through which small and, now in increasing numbers, large investors can invest in a diversified portfolio of stocks, bonds, or a combination of the two.

Visualize a large basket filled with stocks or bonds. Off to the side is a big bucket filled with money—money from small and large investors. Each investor owns a pro-rata share of each stock in the basket. Even the $100-month-investor owns a tiny sliver of each company—akin to a handful of confetti.

With each strand of confetti representing a different company, you can easily see why a mutual fund is considered a less risky way to invest in stocks than owning a few single stocks. If one of the companies in your mutual fund went out of business, you would have to throw away one strand of confetti—but you would still have a handful of confetti representing all the other companies you would still own; you would not have lost all your money. This is why mutual funds are considered the conservative way for small investors to participate in the stock market.

To understand how the world of mutual funds is organized, visualize a group of umbrellas. Each umbrella is known as a family of funds. Each rib on the umbrella represents a separate mutual fund and has the basket of stocks hanging from the tip of that rib. Each basket is well diversified, containing many stocks that often comprise over 100 companies, which means you can reduce your risk by investing in a piece of many companies with as little as $100.

Visualize a golf umbrella of many colors. Think of each color as representing a different category of mutual fund. The red might mean aggressive; the green, growth and income; the blue, income; the yellow, bonds; and the orange, international. An umbrella can have many ribs or just a few. The more ribs on the umbrella, the more funds from which you'll be able to select as your objectives in life change. If you invest in a mutual fund company (or umbrella), you can move your money from fund to fund (rib to rib) with little or no fee as your objectives change throughout your life.

When you invest in a mutual fund, you become a shareholder in the fund and own the companies in the fund through fund shares. Therefore, you own fractional shares that represent multiple companies in the fund.

SELECTING A MUTUAL FUND

With over 9,000 mutual funds from which to choose, you can generally find one that meets your investment objectives and provides a risk level acceptable to you. Mutual funds fall into broad categories.

Bond funds. These funds invest primarily in bonds, sometimes specializing by the entity issuing the bond, and include corporate bonds; government bonds; lower-quality, higher-income corporate and government bonds; and tax-exempt bonds. They are appropriate for those seeking a fixed income with no growth. If interest rates go up, these funds will in all likelihood go down.

Equity-income or growth and income funds. These funds invest in companies with a history of paying dividends and sometimes include government and corporate bonds. They are appropriate for the investor seeking income with a little growth who is not afraid of modest volatility. However, if interest rates go up, these funds will very likely go down a bit.

Balanced funds. These funds contain a relatively fixed percentage of stocks and bonds. They produce income and growth for the investor. If the portfolio contains 50 percent or more in bonds, the fund's value could go down substantially as interest rates rise. However, if the fund contains more stocks than bonds, the total value could actually increase as the stock market rises relative to the amount of stocks versus bonds in the fund. In general, balanced funds provide less dramatic fluctuations than either stock or bond funds separately.

Total return funds. These funds give portfolio managers the flexibility to change the balance among stocks, preferred stocks, or bonds, depending on changing market conditions. They are for the investor seeking a good overall return while minimizing volatility.

Growth funds. These funds invest in companies that pay little or no dividends. They are designed to provide capital appreciation through selecting companies that are expected to grow over time. They are riskier because investors don't receive any money unless the companies do grow and appreciate.

Aggressive growth funds. These are the riskiest of all funds and are very volatile. They provide no income to investors but seek small, aggressive companies on the move. If the fund managers select correctly, the fundholders can make a lot of money. If the fund managers make mistakes, fundholders can lose a lot of money. Aggressive growth funds are, therefore, appropriate for younger investors or those who don't need the return of principal or growth at any particular point in time.

Sector funds. These funds invest in a prespecified industry sector, such as finance, health care, technology, precious metals, natural resources, or real estate. They provide much less diversification than other funds and are more subject to volatility from their reliance on the performance in a particular industry sector. Sector funds are appropriate for the investor who is well informed about a particular industry and is willing to accept the volatility of that particular sector without the balancing offered by more diversification.

> *"U.S. stocks make up only 26% of the world's stocks."*
>
> —*Federation Internationale des Bourses de Valeurs*

Overseas funds.   Global funds invest in stocks from all over the world, including the United States; international and foreign funds exclude the United States from their holdings and are appropriate for the investor who already is invested in a diversified selection of funds in the United States. According to Robert J. Froehlich in *The Three Bears Are Dead!* back in 1970 the U.S. stock market represented approximately 70 percent of the total world market capitalization. In 1998, "with the rapid growth of the equity markets throughout the world, U. S. equities now account for roughly ½ of that total," Froehlich says. "Looked at another way, that means if you limit your portfolio only to U.S. stocks, you are forfeiting the chance to participate in 5 out of every 10 of the world's equity investment opportunities."

It is important to remember that both stocks and bonds will fluctuate. Because of that volatility, it is best to plan to hold your mutual funds five years or longer.

Assessing Your Risk Tolerance

Portfolio balancing is often tied to investors' age, and many times that link is meaningful. However, for boomers playing catch-up it is more appropriate to take a bit more risk than for boomers who have adequately prepared for retirement in their earlier years. Mutual funds are the investment of choice for both groups because even the more volatile funds are more conservative than a smaller portfolio of individual stocks. Thus, aggressive mutual funds are usually a good choice even for 50-year-old boomers. Use Figure 7.1 to help you determine where you fall on the risk continuum: conservative, moderate, or aggressive.

FIGURE 7.1   What's Your Investment Profile?

Your situation and future goals should determine how you invest and which programs best suit your situation. These profiles and suggestions are very broad and should be used for general guidance only. Because of the increased cost of multiple investments, it may be wise to diversify when you have accumulated substantial savings. Use the questions below to help guide you in determining the types of investments most appropriate for your situation.

Low Risk/Low Reward	*High Risk/High Reward*
___I plan to stop working in the next few years.	___I expect to continue working for a long time.
___I'm planning a major purchase (house, car, college tuition) in the next few years.	___I have savings and investments outside the plan.
___I am the only breadwinner in my family.	___I don't mind if my investments have a loss, because I believe it will be made up in the long term.
___I want investments that are safe and stable, even if that means accepting lower rewards.	___My family has another source of income.
	___I want to invest so I can have the most money possible when I leave the state.

If you checked . . .   Then your investment profile is . . .

Most of the boxes in the left column	Conservative
An equal number of boxes in both columns	Moderate
Most of the boxes in the right column	Aggressive

Conservative investors. Generally will put most of their money into high quality, stable options which conserve principal. These options will be a money market fund or a fixed income account which pays interest on the fund balance. There should be no fluctuation of the account value.

Moderate investors. While not wanting to risk all of their investable dollars, they do want to experience some accelerated growth and are

(continued)

FIGURE 7.1 What's Your Investment Profile? *(continued)*

willing to assume some risk of loss as a compromise. These investors could choose a balanced fund which invests in both bonds and stocks. They might also have another fund which guarantees their investment dollars such as a money market account or a fixed income account. A third option would be an index fund investing in large, well capitalized companies. Although the overall value of their accounts might fluctuate somewhat, it should be more stable than a purely growth-oriented approach.

Aggressive investors. Seek high returns on their investment dollars. They understand that by putting money at risk they can command a higher *potential* rate of return . . . though they realize there is no guarantee of their investment. They also tend to have a long-term view of investing. Over the short term, their account balances may actually drop in value. But over time, they believe that they will earn far in excess of what can be made in a "savings" type of account. Alternatives would include a small company stock fund, aggressive growth fund, and an international fund.

Source: State of Georgia Deferred Compensation Plan.

Once you have determined your investment profile, you will be ready to select your mutual funds. If you're the "do-it-yourself" type, you've probably already found that selecting a mutual fund from the 9,000+ available is no easy job. The following criteria can help you select a mutual fund if you want to place your money according to your risk profile and then not worry about it.

CRITERIA FOR SELECTING A MUTUAL FUND

Ponder these four points:

1. The average experience of mutual fund managers industrywide is 4.3 years.
2. The average age for mutual fund managers industrywide is 29.
3. We have not had a normal market correction of a negative 10 percent for a complete year since 1974.

4. If a 29-year-old with 4.3 years of experience is managing your fund and the market does go down 10 percent, will that person have the experience and knowledge to protect your assets?

If you knew your fund existed in 1974, had beat the market during the downturn, and is being managed today by the same system that was used in 1974, would you sleep better at night? If the answer is no, then my logical thought processes and yours don't match and you will need to skip this section and use whatever method suits you to find your fund. On the other hand, if your answer is yes, and you'd be more comfortable with your fund performance during bad markets, read on to learn more about how to find the funds that address the fourth point raised above.

If you want to find funds that perform well in bad markets, go back, not to 1974, but to 1973. The unmanaged S&P 500 stock index went down a total of 40 percent between those two years—the second-worst recorded performance of our stock market since the Great Depression of 1930-31 when the S&P 500 stock index declined over 65 percent. Look for funds whose performance is better than the unmanaged S&P 500 stock index during 1973 and 1974. (See the discussion of the Ibbotson chart in Appendix A).

To avoid the problem of a fund whose performance was created by one person who may have been there once but is not there today, look for a fund managed by a "systems approach" (that is, by multiple managers or by an analytical model that must be followed regardless of the person guiding the fund).

What we are trying to avoid here is the problem illustrated by the Fidelity Magellan fund, which was managed from its inception in the early '70s by its "star manager," Peter Lynch, who left in the early '90s. The fund has had a series of star managers since Lynch left. However, the uninformed investor might review its track record back to the early '70s and decide to invest, not realizing the star responsible for an outstanding performance is no longer there. Records aren't presented on a time line that informs potential investors of the parade of star managers through the years. Therefore, it is essential to say that there are no guarantees available for mutual fund investors, including preservation of principal. Because there are no guarantees whatsoever, it is increasingly important for investors to find funds managed by either a team or by a system instead of by an individual who may be there today and gone tomorrow. Even these funds are subject to many risks, and past performance is never a guarantee of future results.

As Larry Lasser, president of Putnam funds, says in defense of the team management approach, "Stars get sick, they go on vacations, . . . humans have failings." Remember, no fund company is obligated to notify its investors when a fund manager leaves. Investors usually learn of a change in fund management through a newspaper after the fact, if then. If a large pension fund or institutional managers learn of a change to fund managers they don't like, they may remove their money from the fund which will drop in value, leaving small investors to wonder why. The best way to protect yourself from this type of manager risk is to invest in a fund managed by a system, preferably a team-driven fund. This hypothesis is supported by *Barron's* magazine (reported under "Teams Win!" in *Bloomberg Personal*, November/December 1996) research performed using Morningstar's Principia software and database, which separated equity funds into two groups: (1) those that say they are team managed or that have multiple managers, and (2) those that name an individual as manager. "We compared the performance of these two groups over multiple periods ending June 30, 1996. The numbers show that team funds outperformed by significant margins."

According to CDA/Wiesenberger Investment Company, as of December 31, 1997, there were 9,455 mutual funds available from which to select. The database is available by calling CDA/Wiesenberger at 800-232-2285; the cost is about $700 a year. The database permits discovery of team-managed funds; finding funds whose management is driven by a model is more difficult. Take a look at Figure 7.2, which summarizes

---

FIGURE 7.2   Mutual Fund Data from CDA/Wiesenberger (as of 12/31/97)

Total number of mutual funds available	9,455
Total number of mutual funds that began in 1973 or earlier	307
Total number of mutual funds that began in 1973 or earlier with a multiple manager system	15
Total number of mutual funds that began in 1973 or earlier with a minimum annual rate of return of 12% (since that time) and a multiple manager system	11

mutual fund data according to multiple manager funds and according to the criteria outlined above.

The strategy recommended here makes selection of a mutual fund much easier. It is difficult to select from over 9,000 different funds, but selecting from 11 is manageable. The 11 funds that meet my criteria are the following:

Amcap Fund	Investment Company of America
American Mutual Fund	American Century 20th Growth Fund
Dodge & Cox Balanced Fund	American Century 20th Select Fund
Dodge & Cox Stock Fund	New Perspective Fund
Growth Fund of America	Washington Mutual Investors Fund
Income Fund of America	

Of the 11 funds, 2 are in the Dodge and Cox family of 3 funds; 2 are in the American Century 20th family of 9 funds; and 7 are in the American family of 28 funds. Seven are front loads and four are no loads.

The funds managed by Dodge and Cox can be reached at P.O. Box 9051, Boston, MA 02205-9051; 800-621-3979. Each fund is managed by a committee of eight to ten members whose tenure with the company averages about 20 years per person.

American Century Services Corp. can be reached at P.O. Box 419200, Kansas City, MO 64141-6200; 800-345-2021. Its funds are managed by teams but no length of service of team members nor exact number of team members was provided in the fund literature.

The remaining seven funds are in the American family with the following information about the teams:

Fund	Number of Team Members	Average Tenure per Person
Amcap	5	24 years
American Mutual	5	30 years
Growth Fund of America	6	26 years
Income Fund of America	7	19 years
Investment Company of America	9	25 years
New Perspective Fund	5	28 years
Washington Mutual Investors Fund	7	23 years

The American family of funds has been called by *Mutual Fund* magazine "the giant nobody knows." In its September 1997 issue, *Mutual Fund* wonders whether the company's reticence is hiding mediocre performance. *Barron's* magazine January 1998 issue reports that when the Dow dropped 5.6 percent during the October 15–November 15, 1997 downturn, Washington Mutual Investors Fund slipped only 2.6 percent. Both magazines emphasize that the team approach used by the fund limits the problem of manager turnover, which now is pervasive in the industry. *Mutual Fund* says: "If one person leaves, it's no big deal."

Putnam is a fund family that realized in the early 1980s the benefit of team-managed funds after being in business since 1937, during which time its funds were managed by stars. Larry Lasser was charged with the task of converting the company to a team-managed approach in 1984. Putnam has "staked its success on keeping its managers on a short leash, carefully pruning the list of stocks from which the teams get to select," according to *Fortune*. President Lasser says, "There are 7,500 mutual funds out there [in 1996]; do you think there are 7,500 stars to manage them? Let me tell you, I don't think there are even 750." *SmartMoney* of January 1998, in its article entitled "My Way or the Highway," reports that Lasser runs Putnam with a heavy hand, "complete with shrink appointments for prospective employees, and intervention sessions for underperforming fund managers . . . and so far, it seems to be working."

While Putnam can't demonstrate results back to 1973's bear market, it can demonstrate impressive results during 1987's "Black Monday" and in 1990 when the S&P 500 closed down for the year. If you believe that the market is in an upswing with the potential for several small dips along the way and that a 10 percent or more annual downturn is probably not in sight for about ten years, you may wish to consider Putnam for team-managed funds as well.

Advantage of System-Managed Funds

Companies other than those noted here are attempting to systematize their fund management. They don't have teams managing their funds, but they have created a somewhat "people-proof system" by making stock and bond picking analytical and by routinizing decision making through the use of a model.

The system usually exists in the research department and the criteria are strictly implemented. The companies use sophisticated analytical models that pursue objective (as opposed to subjective) conclusions about holdings that fit each company's criteria. From the resulting and much narrowed list (perhaps from 5,000 down to 300), the one or two fund managers make their selections. By virtue of their system, the companies argue, major errors are screened out before the fund managers even see the list.

Two fund families in particular (AIM and Pioneer) are adamant about their respective systems and the reliability of results over time. The AIM family of funds, which began in 1967 and merged in 1997 with INVESCO, reports its management model is earnings driven. There is a "discipline" AIM brags on billboards throughout Atlanta and on TV commercials. It reviews the earnings of stocks every quarter.

Simplistically speaking, stocks whose earnings were equal to or greater than management expected (earnings surprise) in a given quarter can be available for purchase by portfolio managers. If, however, there is an earnings "disappointment" (earnings were less than management expected), stocks must be sold out of the portfolio whether the portfolio manager wants to or not.

AIM research has found that when an earnings surprise occurs, the stock price of a company will go up three quarters in a row after that 80 percent of the time. On the flip side, if there is an earnings disappointment, the stock price will go down three quarters in a row 80 percent of the time. Admittedly, some refining criteria are related to the size of companies and their dividend-paying history, but, nevertheless, management decision making is systematized so investors can hope that the track record of the past has some relevance as they move into the future, though past performance is no guarantee of future results.

The Pioneer Company began in 1928 under the tutelage of its founder, Philip Carret, who created a value-oriented model by which Pioneer funds have been managed since the beginning. Of course, the model has been refined and updated through the years, but the model drives the research department to screen out any stocks that cannot be purchased under book value. Pioneer brags that its research is original research, not purchased from any of the many research firms. It also says that because of this research approach, it often finds wonderful companies whose stock price is under book value because other major mutual fund companies and brokerage houses haven't found those companies yet. Pioneer's research department requires that anyone working there use the model developed by Mr. Carret and perfected through the years.

Steve Long of Pioneer says, "Because of our system of detecting companies that are undervalued, the investor can be assured that we have purchased what we believe to be companies with potential to grow just because we bought them right; not because we think they will do something like offer a new product or service in the future to make the growth occur. The stock price only has to grow to its *current* book value for our investors to make money."

This system of purchasing undervalued equities usually leads to lowered risk. *Barron's* of January 1998 reported the Pioneer Fund to be one of the ten least risky funds for 1997.

LOAD FUNDS

A load is the fee charged investors by which a mutual fund company gets reimbursed for its distribution and marketing expenses. All front-end load (i.e., up-front fees called Class A shares) mutual funds offer a volume discount feature often referred to as "break points." The more dollars you have to invest, the lower the percentage charged as a front load. The following table indicates roughly the same percentage decreases in front-load funds industrywide as the dollar amounts increase.

Volume Discount Feature

Amount of Investment	*Front-End Load %*
Less than $50,000	5.75
$ 50,000 but less than $100,000	4.50
$100,000 but less than $250,000	3.50
$250,000 but less than $500,000	2.50
$500,000 but less than $1,000,000	2.00
Over $1,000,000	0

Load funds aren't necessarily bad. It would not be smart, however, to invest in a front-end load fund one year and cash out of it one or two years later. Investors planning to cash out in a short period of time would be wiser to use a fund with neither a front-end nor back-end load. Look instead for a no-load fund.

Investors planning to invest long term, however, would find a front-end load fund less expensive in the long run. By biting the bullet and paying the load up front, investors' biggest costs are fixed and spread out over all the years they hold the fund. If the fund's annual operating expenses are lower than the industry average (see the chart in Figure 7.3 for industry averages), it would be a better move than even a no-load fund whose annual operating expenses are above the industry average.

Another type of load fund is a back-end load, a fund with Class B shares. Instead of paying a fee to buy the mutual fund, investors pay a fee to get out of the mutual fund within a certain number of years (usually seven). Withdrawals of up to 10 percent a year can be taken without incurring a penalty. After seven or another specified number of years, investors pay no fee to get out. In the table below is the schedule of declining surrender penalties generally assessed.

Number of Years in Fund	1	2	3	4	5	6	7
% deducted	5	4	4	3	2	1	0

Class B shares usually have higher annual fees than Class A shares, but those fees are reduced to match the lower Class A annual fees after the surrender penalty period has expired.

Class C shares, sometimes referred to as "level load" funds, deduct no fee on investing and 1 percent if liquidated within 12 months. Instead, they generally deduct about 1 percent every year you own the fund. This fee, called a 12b-1 fee, is added to the annual operating expenses. For funds whose 12b-1 fee is lower than 1 percent, be sure the total annual operating expenses are lower than the industry average.

> *"Age and money are the things that drive people to advice."*
>
> —*Vanguard's chief executive and president, John Brennan, quoting an unnamed Merrill Lynch executive,* The Wall Street Journal, *Jan. 29, 1998*

NO-LOAD FUNDS

A common misconception about no-load funds is that no costs are associated with them. Both a load and a 12b-1 fee are considered ways for a mutual fund company to obtain reimbursement for marketing and distribution expenses. Even no-load funds have marketing and distribution expenses for which they must be reimbursed. Otherwise, how would they pay for their TV commercials or other media advertising?

When you inspect the expense disclosure page of a prospectus, look for how the fund is recapturing its expenses for marketing and distribution. The 12b-1 fee is the straightforward way for the reimbursement to occur. If there is no 12b-1 fee, look for the reimbursement in the "miscellaneous expense" category. If it is not disclosed there, you can fairly safely assume the company is recovering its cost in the transaction fees associated with buying and selling the securities in the fund. This buying and selling, which is part of the way portfolio managers make money for investors, is characterized on a fund's financial statement (also in the prospectus) as "portfolio turnover percentage."

From one fund to another, the annual portfolio turnover percentage can vary from 10 to 300 percent or more. The higher the turnover, the more fees are being taken from your fund and used for expenses for which no disclosure is required—presumably some of which could be marketing and distribution.

In addition to marketing and distribution expenses, the category called "operating expenses" covers all overhead expenses for such things as office and furniture rental, telephone service, mail, administration, legal costs, accounting, travel, and so on. Operating expenses also include compensation to the persons managing the stock or bond portfolios. Operating expenses are deducted from your account as a percentage of your total account balance on a daily basis, but these deductions are never shown on your statement. The numbers on your statement already have all fees deducted.

Absolutely and unequivocally, no mutual fund in existence has zero annual operating expenses. Here's a hint: If you see a zero in one or more areas of the expense allocations in the prospectus, turn quickly to the financial statement and examine the portfolio turnover percentage. It is the total operating expense percentage charged each year in conjunction with the portfolio turnover percentage that lets you correctly assess the annual fees being deducted and will thus have an impact on your total return. And even then you will have to make an educated guess.

Most front-end load and back-end load funds also charge a 12b-1 fee annually. The difference in the 12b-1 fee is related to how quickly the fund management company gets its marketing and distribution costs reimbursed. If, for example, a fund charges a front-end load, the 12b-1 fee will be lower than in a back-end load fund. If a fund charges a back-end load, the 12b-1 fee will be a bit higher than in the front-end load fund but will be reduced to the "base operating expense fee" charged by the Class A share structure after the penalty period for withdrawal is up. If, however, there is no front-end or back-end load charged and the fund company is not trying to hide its marketing and distribution expenses in the miscellaneous category or under portfolio turnover, the 12b-1 fee will generally be higher than the front-end or back-end load . . . and it will never go down.

As a General Rule:
How to Decide Which Expense Structure Is Best for You

Three points to consider when deciding what type of fund is best for you:

1. Decide how long you will hold the fund. If you're going to hold it for one to three and a half years, choose Class C shares or no-load fee structure.

2. If you're going to hold the fund for more than three and a half years and you don't have $50,000 to invest, choose Class B shares (back-end load).

3. If you're going to hold the fund for longer than three and a half years and you can get at least a $50,000 break point, choose Class A shares (front-end load).

Fees have always been difficult to understand as well as much of the other information about mutual funds. According to *Bloomberg News* as reported in the *Charlotte Observer* of April 1998, "The rule calls for two new documents to tell investors about a mutual fund's goals, risks, fees, and performance . . . which is mandatory . . . for all funds starting December 1, 1998. . . . The profile also will have a summary of the fund fees, risks, and investment objectives."

DECIDING WHAT'S BEST FOR YOU:
LOAD OR NO-LOAD? ADVICE OR NO ADVICE?

"Something's wrong with me, Grandma," sighed a
young lady. "I've been a bridesmaid twice; I caught
the bouquet, too, but I'm still single."
"Next time," advised Grandma, "don't reach for the
flowers; reach for the best man."

—*Public Speaker's Treasure Chest*

The decision is really not between load or no-load. The decision is between advice or no advice. There comes a time in the investing lives of busy people when they are reluctant to take on the entire responsibility for managing their total portfolio. It is usually when they have aged a bit and realize the funds they have are the only ones they will have for the rest of their life. This is happening with increasing frequency among boomers.

On one side of a dichotomy in the mutual fund industry are funds whose fees are shared with brokers (typically called load); on the other side are funds whose fees are not shared (typically called no-load).

Those for Whom No-Load Funds Are Appropriate

No-load funds are for investors who truly are do-it-yourselfers and who intend to watch the funds daily and, if they feel it necessary, move the money from one fund to another. These moves would be frequent, maybe several times within a year.

No-load funds would also be appropriate for those who have hired a broker and are paying an annual wrap fee (ranging from 1 percent to 3 percent per year) for the broker to move frequently from one no-load fund to another.

It certainly would not make sense for anyone who intends to move the money around within three years to use load funds. The circumstances under which a move from one fund to another would occur are dictated by the adviser's opinion that economic conditions, fund performance, fund manager changes, or other technical factors might be set to impact the fund's performance negatively. The move would be aimed at cutting losses and maximizing gains, an approach generally referred to as "timing."

To look at your real rate of return in this type of adviser-client arrangement, you would obviously need to deduct the adviser's fee from the gross return to arrive at your net return.

Those for Whom Load Funds Are Appropriate

Load funds are designed for the investor who wants an adviser's help at the least cost. Most financial planners or brokers who use load funds don't charge a wrap fee because the fund company is sharing some of its annual operating expense (usually about .002, i.e., .2 percent) per year with the adviser.

Load funds are more appropriate for the investor who plans to use an asset allocation model. Under this plan, the investor would, with the help of the adviser, make a decision about diversifying his or her portfolio with a prescribed amount of money into each of several funds and leave that money invested for the long haul (at least four years) before moving it to another fund. And when the money is moved to another fund, that fund would be within the same family of funds, thereby avoiding a repeat of fees that would otherwise occur if the money were moved to another family.

The circumstances under which money is moved into a different arrangement of funds are dictated by a change in a client's objectives. That is, a client might be pursuing a growth goal for a few years prior to retirement and, at retirement, would need to begin withdrawing income.

Load Versus No-Load Trend in the Industry

According to Robert McGough in a *Wall Street Journal* article, "The Comeback Kid of Mutual Funds: The Load" (January 29, 1998), the "unstoppable 'no-load' fund revolution in which investors would save money on brokers by picking their own mutual funds . . . has been moving in the opposite direction." Scudder, Stein Roe, Pilgrim Baxter, to name a few, are converting all or some of their funds to load status "to sell through brokers and other financial 'intermediaries.' Investors have a lot more money to handle . . . and as they have gotten older, their financial problems have become more complicated," says McGough. Paul Hondros, president of Pilgrim Baxter, which handles the PBHG funds, says, "In many cases, it's more money than they [investors] thought they would ever have. There's a certain amount of apprehension that goes along with the thought that it's their retirement savings: It has to last the rest of their lives." This drives people to advice. "Advice is not going away. If anything, we believe it's a growth area," says Hondros.

Further evidence that people are moving away from no-load funds is the fact that 40 percent of the money that went to Vanguard in 1997 came from individuals directly. The balance of the money came from retirement plans or through advisers who wrapped the entire account with a 1 to 3 percent annual fee. McGough reports that even Fidelity and Vanguard have made "concessions to the advice wave."

Fidelity now offers funds that have front-end loads paid to brokers and Vanguard is considering offering advice; "for instance, for $500, a Vanguard-employed adviser will give an investor one-time advice on 'asset allocation' among different types of mutual funds," says Brennan, Vanguard's chief executive and president.

Suppose you have opted for the no-load, wrap-fee arrangement with an adviser. Suppose your adviser quits, retires, gets sick, goes on vacation, or just has a couple of bad days! What will happen to your investments? Who is designated to take over the management of your funds?

If Not a Team, a System of Management

If your fund is not managed by multiple managers or a team, make sure an analytical system or decision-making model is in place and must be adopted by every succeeding manager of the fund. Make sure the model has been in place since 1973 (or at least through a couple of down years) and that it has produced results that outperform the unmanaged S&P 500—especially in the down years.

As you evaluate annual expenses charged by a fund, it may be helpful to know the industry averages as of December 31, 1997, as shown in Figure 7.3.

FIGURE 7.3   Annual Industrywide Expense Ratios

Category	Industry Average (%)[1]
Growth	1.51
Growth and income	1.43
International/Global	1.89
Equity-income	1.34[2]
Balanced	1.40
Taxable bond	1.21
Tax-exempt bond	1.13
Money market	0.59[3]

Source: The American Funds Group, using data gathered from (1) CDA/Wiesenberger, (2) Morningstar, and (3) IBC/Donoghue's *Money-Fund Report.*

INDEX FUNDS

Simply stated, an index fund is a mutual fund consisting of an equal number of shares of the companies that make up the index. For example, the S&P 500 stock index is made up of the Fortune 500 companies. If you like the idea of owning the largest 500 companies in our country, consider an index fund.

These funds are simple to manage. No decision making is required. No research is required. No adjustments are made for market or economic fluctuations. The funds are always fully invested. And because no management is required, the fees are very low.

Over the past 20 years, with the unprecedented growth of the stock market, index funds have done well. Because they do not have the benefit of management, they are unable to reposition investments as a defensive measure against potential market downturns. In a downtrending market, however, index funds usually do not perform as well as managed funds.

The currently popular index funds are "unmanaged"—that is, if a company's stock goes up in a year, no one decides to sell while it is high and wait till it drops lower to buy it back and thus increase the number of shares owned. Contrast the unmanaged approach with the "managed" approach. If, for example, 100 shares valued at $40 a share, went up to $50 a share, and then went back down to $40 where they started, the unmanaged portfolio would have gone from $4,000 up to $5,000 and back down to $4,000. In a managed approach, the management system would probably trigger a sale at $50 a share and thus create $5,000 in cash. When the stock dropped to $40 a share, the managers could buy it back to own now a block of 125 shares. Then when the price went back to $50 a share, the 125 shares would create a value of $6,250. However, the more the fund managers buy and sell within a fund within one year, the greater the tax owed on the capital gain generated.

Planning for mutual funds in your portfolio.   For the conservative investor, mutual funds provide the prudent vehicle for investing in stocks and bonds. Through mutual funds the investor can own a wide array of stocks for as little as $50 and be assured of diversification. Mutual funds also eliminate the problem of thinking about buying and selling individual securities. Some advisers work exclusively with mutual funds and your money. Many are paid by the mutual fund through the load and 12b-1 fee, so you would not actually "feel" the payment of fees for advice. Other advisers receive not only load and 12b-1 fees but also annual fees ranging from 1 to 3 percent a year on your entire portfolio. You would "feel" that fee as you would have to sign an agreement authorizing the fund to liquidate shares of your account to pay the adviser's fee or you would receive an invoice directly from the adviser.

HOW TO SELECT *YOUR* MUTUAL FUND

You've read this chapter and say, "Okay, I'm ready to invest and I like the concept of a system of management. Which particular fund is the right one for me?"

- First, clarify your objective. If you are playing catch-up for retirement planning, you need growth and you need it as safely as you can get it. Growth comes from stocks and real estate. Safety comes from diversification. To get both at one time, invest in mutual funds.
- Determine your risk tolerance. If you are targeting an average annual rate of return of 12 percent, you'll need to be able to toler-

ate a downturn of 12 percent in your portfolio. If you want a 20 percent-a-year return, you'll need to be able to tolerate a 20 percent downturn.

- Select the families of mutual funds whose systems of management you understand and with which you feel comfortable. Make sure the management system will allow you to sleep at night and have peace of mind, even though you realize there are no guarantees. At this stage of your life, no investment is worth making if you'll worry about it.
- Within the family of funds, choose funds that match your risk tolerance. Look for a fund whose long-term performance has met your risk-considered target rate of return determined by your objectives. Be sure the fund performance has factored in the bad years of 1973–74.
- Diversify among asset classes; that is, own large, medium-sized, and small company funds. Also diversify globally. The farther away from retirement you are, the more funds with small companies and foreign companies you will be able to own. If you are within three years of retirement, own no more than 15 percent in small company funds and no more than 20 percent outside the United States. Only add bonds if you are nervous about volatility or when you actually stop working and need income. If you need income within two years, position your assets to have 40 to 60 percent in bond funds.
- If you are more than three years from retirement, try to gain a comfort level while pushing yourself to take a bit more risk. That is, strive to own up to 30 percent in funds containing small companies and up to 40 percent in funds that contain foreign stocks. As long as you are in funds that are system managed and have results to show that they have survived the bad years of 1973–74, your overall risk will be minimized. So go for the returns!
- Now, invest the amount determined by your Retirement Income Calculator in Chapter 4 and don't look at your fund performances every month. Force yourself to look no more frequently than once a quarter. To make your investing easier, have your investments automatically deducted from your checking account monthly. This will insure that you accomplish your retirement investment goal and that your intended investment won't be accidentally overlooked at the end of the month.

Pulling Together Your Retirement Plan

*"The Eiffel Tower is the Empire State Building
after taxes."*

—Anonymous

TAX-WISE STRATEGIES FOR THE
RETIREMENT-BOUND BOOMER

There's good news and bad news about making money on your investments. The good news is that you are making money! The bad news is that you will pay taxes on the money you make if you don't plan carefully. The money you earn on your investments is reported to you on an IRS form called a 1099. The best alternative to never having to pay taxes on investment gains—the ideal—is to not pay taxes on your investment gains until you withdraw the money for personal use. The worst alternative is to pay taxes on the gains every year before you reinvest the money.

You make money on your investments under each alternative, but the return you realize in your pocket is greatest if you pay no taxes. The next best is to pay the taxes later, and the final is to pay taxes each year.

142

Taxable Investments

If you have no way to place your investments into a tax-deferred vehicle, you will receive a Form 1099 and have to pay taxes annually at your regular income tax rate on interest, dividends, and short-term capital gains. So if you are in the 31, 36, or 39.6 percent marginal bracket, your investment income will be taxed appropriately. Because you'll pay taxes on your gains, you'll have an annual return that is lowered by the rate of your tax bracket.

If you have held your investment for not less than 12 months nor more than 18 months, your taxes will be calculated at the long-term capital gains rate of 28 percent. If you have held the investment for 18 months or longer, your taxes on your profit will be capped at 20 percent if your bracket is more than 15 percent and at 10 percent if your bracket is 15 percent or under.

Examples of the investments subject to this type of taxation are interest-bearing alternatives primarily purchased through a bank, and dividends and short-term gains on stocks, bonds, and mutual funds commonly purchased through a brokerage firm.

Tax-Deferred Investments

To the extent your investments are held in individual retirement accounts (IRAs), 401(k) accounts, pension, profit-sharing or other "qualified" plans, or by insurance companies through annuities, you will be able to reinvest all your interest, dividends, and capital gains but pay no taxes when you reinvest it. You'll have to pay taxes on the gains you've earned through the years only when you withdraw your investment.

For years investors have thought they would be in a lower income tax bracket when they retired. For that reason they never hesitated to invest as much as possible into tax-deferred plans, thinking their taxes would be lower when they withdrew the money in the future. Today, because of "bracket creep," many are paying taxes at the same rate when they retire as before. Although you may question the reason for investing for tax-deferred growth, it *is* the better way. Consider this example.

Mary invested $3,600 into her 401(k) plan and left it there for 15 years and paid no taxes on the gains. Over that time, she earned 10 percent tax-deferred on the money, bringing her total to $15,038. She withdrew all $15,038 after 15 years and paid federal taxes of 28 percent and state taxes of 6 percent. She had $9,925 left.

Joe invested the same $3,600 in an account earning 10 percent and every year paid federal taxes of 28 percent and state taxes of 6 percent. Every year he paid taxes on the 10 percent interest he earned, leaving 6.6 percent actual after-tax earnings. At the end of 15 years, Joe had $9,389 in his account.

Thus, Mary ended up with $535 more in her pocket even though both had invested exactly the same amount. The only difference was how the taxes were paid. The greater the returns, the greater the impact of deferring the taxes; and the tax advantage is even better if you can leave your money invested longer.

Tax-Free or Tax-Favored Investing

Only a very few ways are available that allow you to reinvest your interest, dividends, and capital gains with no taxation and then to withdraw the dollars you invested plus those you gained through the years with no taxation. These investments are only available through municipal bonds or life insurance products and the life insurance products must be structured very carefully.

A municipal bond provides you with tax-free interest and the return of principal when the bond matures. Without the reinvestment of the interest, your investment will not grow.

To have a tax-free or tax-favored investment that will grow, you must purchase a life insurance policy and place as many dollars into the cash accumulation account as possible. See Figure 6.1 in Chapter 6 for a summary of the benefits of life insurance products as retirement-planning vehicles. In effect, you will be overfunding your policy by paying the premium due and adding dollars that you can direct, if you use a variable universal life policy, into mutual fund–type subaccounts and benefit from the gains (as well as potential losses) of the stock markets. If we assume your cash accumulation account grows faster than the premium cost, you will have at retirement a sum of money for personal spending. But just as with other investments in the stock market, there are no guarantees.

Life insurance contracts have for years allowed you to withdraw the dollars you paid in premiums as return of premium and therefore not taxed. The contracts also allowed you to borrow tax-free your earnings on your account at a low interest rate (since you were borrowing your own money). As long as your policy remains in effect, the money you withdraw is not taxed. But the moment you withdraw so much that the money left is insufficient to pay the death benefit required by the policy contract, you will receive a 1099 on all the income you've received above the amount you paid into the policy.

This investment is very popular with boomers in their 40s. It's a great way for a healthy forty-year-old to aggressively pursue retirement funding by using tax-deferred growth and tax-free or tax-favored withdrawal. For smokers or boomers with health problems, however, this option is not good because the high cost of insurance eats away at the potential investment growth.

In selecting a variable universal life insurance contract, evaluate carefully the company's overall cost of insurance, its mortality charges, and its other fees inside the contract.

Congress may some day in the future disallow continued funding of variable universal life insurance as withdrawals are tax-free. However, because the insurance company lobby is so strong, it is unlikely that Congress will retroactively disallow the tax-free or tax-favored component of this investment, although anything is possible. So be forewarned if you pursue this alternative.

TAX-DEFERRED STRATEGIES FOR INVESTING

According to the 1997 edition of the *ICI Mutual Fund Fact Book,* IRA assets throughout the nation have more than doubled in the past five years. Two new IRA account opportunities are now available as the result of the Taxpayer Relief Act of 1997—the Roth IRA and the Education IRA. Both plans allow you to

- make nondeductible contributions,
- enjoy the benefit of having the account accumulate tax-free, and
- make tax- and penalty-free withdrawals under certain conditions (see qualified purpose distribution later in this chapter).

Regular deductible or nondeductible $2,000 IRAs, SEPs, SIMPLEs, money purchase pension plans, profit-sharing plans, and 401(k) and

403(b) plans still exist. But under the 1997 tax law, Congress also made several changes to regular IRAs that took effect in 1998 and made them even more attractive: (1) the income limits for making deductible contributions to a regular IRA have been raised and will continue to increase each year until 2007; (2) spouses have been "delinked" for determining the deductibility of contributions so that the spouse of an active participant in an employer-sponsored retirement plan is able to make a deductible IRA contribution as long as the couple's combined income is less than $160,000 a year; and (3) prior to age 59½, penalty-free withdrawals are allowed for first-time home purchases (lifetime cap of up to $10,000) and higher-education expenses.

Following are discussions of the newer plans and the provisions that characterize them.

Roth IRAs

The hottest topic coming out of the Taxpayer Relief Act of 1997 is the Roth IRA. The primary feature of the Roth IRA is that withdrawals can be made completely tax-free after the five taxable-year period beginning with the first taxable year for which a contribution was made to a Roth IRA *and* if one of the following four circumstances applies to the owner of the Roth IRA:

1. Aged 59½
2. Death
3. Disability
4. Qualified special circumstance (discussed later)

The maximum contribution to a Roth IRA is the same $2,000 per person as the old IRA, reduced by any contribution to another IRA. Positive features include a provision that allows contributions after age 70½ (if contributor is still employed) and no requirements for minimum withdrawals after age 70½.

As you might expect, if you are "rich," you can't have a Roth IRA. For this purpose, "rich" is defined as having an adjusted gross income of $95,000 to $110,000 for singles and $150,000 to $160,000 for married taxpayers filing jointly.

IRA conversions to a Roth. You can convert a regular IRA to a Roth IRA in a year that your income, not counting the rollover, is less than $100,000 without paying the 10 percent penalty for early withdrawal. Then if you meet the five-year holding period and other qualifications, you can receive your IRA tax-free after retirement. You do have to pay tax on any taxable portion of your IRA; thus, if you're in a 28 percent federal income tax bracket and you convert $10,000 from a regular IRA to a Roth IRA, you'll owe $2,800 in federal taxes in the year during which the conversion was made. The taxes may come from sources other than the conversion or they can be deducted.

Planning idea. Don't automatically assume a conversion is beneficial to you. You'll need to compute the effective reduction in your IRA caused by the current taxes you have to pay. Compare the after-tax growth with the tax-free growth currently available to you. Evaluate the tax-free income available under the Roth when you retire. In each case there will be a different answer.

If you are eligible for both, carefully consider your options. In general, the younger you are, the more beneficial the Roth. Conversely, the closer you are to retirement, the more beneficial the tax deductible IRA.

Further, you must consider your tax bracket. If you expect to be in a lower tax bracket in the future, the tax-deductible IRA may be better to keep. As for a conversion, if you are currently in a higher tax bracket, taxes may severely erode your principal, making the Roth conversion less attractive.

As this is a provision that was only effective beginning in 1998, you will be well advised to consult your tax adviser for help.

A qualified special purpose distribution. References are made often to a "qualified special purpose distribution" in the new tax law. This is a special distribution and is not subject to the 10 percent penalty incurred if you make withdrawals before age 59½. Exceptions that have been in place for a while are disability, death, substantially equal periodic payments, certain medical expenses exceeding 7.5 percent of income, medical insurance for the unemployed, and educational expenses. These are not specifically the qualified special purpose distribution.

The only current qualified special purpose distribution allows penalty-free, but taxable, withdrawals with a $10,000 lifetime cap for the purchase of a home by a first-time homebuyer. The homebuyer can be you, your spouse, child, grandchild, or ancestor. The distribution is taxed at your normal income tax rate.

Planning idea.   The best way to make a down payment for your home may not be through a qualified special purpose distribution. For example, imagine that you take $10,000 from your IRA at age 45 for a home. Assume you pay 33 percent, or $3,300, in federal and state taxes on this money, leaving you $6,700 for the down payment. If you had left the $10,000 in your IRA and if it had earned 10 percent for the next 20 years, you would have $67,275 more in your retirement nest egg. From this nest egg you would have been able to withdraw 7 percent, or $4,709 *a year.* Further, your nest egg would still be intact for your future needs and for your estate.

Just because this distribution is an available option, don't think it's the best one for you. Consult your tax or financial adviser for assistance with this complex set of provisions.

Education IRAs

A new type of IRA has been established that looks great on the surface but could have some long-range adverse complications. The Education IRA allows up to $500 to be deposited to a child's account starting in 1998. The deposit is not tax deductible, but no tax is paid on the earnings until they're withdrawn. If the funds are withdrawn to pay for college, including postgraduate work, they are withdrawn tax-free. Simple so far.

The complications start here. The $500 can be deposited by anybody— parents, grandparents, friends, and even conceivably the children themselves. However, only $500 can be made on behalf of any one child each year, no matter how many people contribute. You must be careful to coordinate this with all potential donors.

There are also income limits for the donors. The $500 limit is phased out if the single contributor's income is between $95,000 and $110,000 ($150,000 and $160,000 for married taxpayers filing joint.)

Planning idea.   If your income exceeds the limits noted above and you still want to contribute, arrange for someone else who qualifies to make the contribution.

No contribution can be made in a year when a contribution has been made for the beneficiary to a state tuition program. Other restrictions exist for government-sponsored scholarships and learning tax credits also made available by the government. So, like so many other government programs, it is difficult to determine what's best for you.

If you don't use the deposited money for educational purposes the withdrawals are subject to the 10 percent early withdrawal penalty. If the money isn't used for the beneficiary by the time he or she reaches 30, the entire amount must be withdrawn subject to tax plus the 10 percent penalty, although the IRA can be rolled over to another Education IRA for a different beneficiary in the same family.

Don't plan for an Education IRA without exploring all of its potential aspects. Also, be aware that $500 a year probably won't cover the entire cost of a child's college expenses. In *Live Long & Profit,* I published a chart showing how much you will need to fund your child's college expenses. (See Chapter 3 for a reprint of that chart.)

SIMPLE IRAs for Small Businesses

New tax-deferred retirement plans for small businesses called SIMPLE (Savings Incentive Match Plans for Employees) plans were created in 1997 and are now available for businesses with fewer than 100 employees. The plan must include all employees who made more than $5,000 a year in the two previous years.

SIMPLE account contributions are tax deferred. Employees can elect to defer a percentage of their income to an IRA-type account and are able to contribute a maximum of $6,000 a year, an amount to be indexed for inflation.

Employers must match employee-made contributions under one of two alternative formulas. The employer can match dollar-for-dollar up to 3 percent of a participating employee's compensation. As a second alternative, the employer can make a 2 percent nonelective contribution for all eligible employees. All contributions made on behalf of employees by the employer are fully vested immediately.

SIMPLEs are not subject to nondiscrimination rules for top-heavy plans and should have little or no administrative costs and any fees associated with the plan are usually structured so that the employee pays his or her own fees. Balances can be transferred from one SIMPLE account to another or from a SIMPLE to an IRA after two years of participation in the SIMPLE plan. Early withdrawals will have a 25 percent penalty for the first two years and a 10 percent penalty thereafter until the employee is 59½.

Most mutual fund companies have developed prototype plans to help small businesses establish their plans with fees generally running about $10 per year deducted from the employee's fund.

SMART STRATEGIES FOR THE RETIREMENT-BOUND BOOMER

Why a Financial Adviser?

In the final analysis, the most important responsibility of a financial adviser is to help you reach your long-term goals. A common mistake of many investors is not staying with their investment plans over the long haul. This is understandable given the wide variety of investment choices available and the accessibility of financial information. Data show that individual investors have not done well when trying to select the right time to sell and the right time to buy back within their own portfolios. Figure 8.1 reflects the performance of selected funds versus the actual performance of shareholders of those funds over a five-year period ending May 31, 1994. The study shows that if the investor had remained invested over the entire five-year period, their return would have been substantially better than when investors moved their money in and out of the funds.

The value that a financial adviser can add to the investment process is potentially significant and has been analyzed. Dalbar published the results

---

FIGURE 8.1   Investments Do Well, Investors Don't
              Over Five Years

Investment returns	+12.5% per year
Investor returns	− 2.2% per year

Source: Morningstar, Inc. Returns are based on 219 growth mutual funds that supplied quarterly net asset and performance returns for the five-year period ending May 31, 1994. The dollar-weighted return is based on the internal rate of return of the growth funds' cash flow.

of their research in *Quantitative Analysis of Investor Behavior,* December 1995, which showed that over a ten-year period, investors who did not use an adviser experienced a total return of +89.58 percent in their equity fund portfolios, while those using an adviser had +101.77 percent total return. The results of this study indicate that investors obtain higher returns when working through financial advisers than when investing on their own. According to the study, investors were more likely to hold onto their investments in market declines when the advice and reassurance of a professional adviser were available. The study shows that advisers add real economic value by altering investor behavior. Advisers don't have to select better investments to be successful. Rather, they prove their worth by convincing investors to invest and to remain invested for the long haul.

Potential returns for patient investors are certainly there. Consider this analysis: From January 1, 1987, to December 31, 1996, the S&P 500, a common barometer for stock market performance, had an average annual total return of 15.3 percent for someone fully invested for all 2,529 days the market was open. (Remember: Past performance is not a guarantee of future results.)

By missing the 10 best days, the return would have dropped to 11 percent per year. However, by missing the 20 biggest, positive days—less than 1 percent of all the trading days—the average return would have been cut nearly in half to 8.1 percent. If the investor missed the 30 best days, the return would have dropped to 5.6 percent, and if the investor missed the 40 best days, the return would have been only 3.3 percent. So, it pays to stay fully invested, and if the adviser helps you do that, the adviser is worth their fee.

Diversification—What to Expect

> *"Success seems to be largely a matter of hanging on after others have let go."*
>
> —*William Feather from* Great Thoughts, Funny Sayings

When planning investment portfolios, be conscious of your risk tolerance—your ability to tolerate negative returns. We all know investments go up and down. To make sure you can sleep at night, you should structure your portfolio so that all of your assets don't go down at the same time. But remember they won't go up at the same time either.

In the 1996–97 U.S. equities market, we saw returns for the S&P 500 in the 20 to 30 percent range. If you happened to own a mutual fund containing smaller companies or companies outside the United States and your return was not as high, you should not be overly concerned; compare your fund's performance with the index of smaller or non-U.S. companies. At such times, remind yourself that the original reason for diversifying was so all your assets wouldn't perform the same at all times. In other words, it was by design.

Think of diversification this way: If you were to plant the same flower all over your yard throughout the year, it would tend to grow and bloom at the same time. But if you were to plant different types of flowers with different blooming cycles and conditions, the chances of your having something blooming in your yard all year long would be much better. If you could match the perfect flower to the time of year, then you would have the perfect garden blooming all year round.

This analogy indicates why advisers discourage impatient investors from moving slower-performing funds at any point in time to faster-performing ones. The idea is to have good performance, but not peak performance, in your investments all year round. If you become impatient and are tempted to move your investments, it would be like pulling up those plants and replanting them at a different time of year. You could miss the blooming cycle for the plants you pulled up. And you would likely have already missed the full bloom of the plant that just produced the biggest flower.

Think about this analogy when you become itchy and want to move your money around. Research shows it won't work in the long run.

POINTERS ABOUT INVESTING IN GENERAL

"All great achievements require time."

—David Joseph Schwartz

If you are starting late, certain pointers can maximize your investment success and minimize your investment failure, saving you valuable time and helping you avoid disasters.

Inflation has been with us since 1954. It is likely to be with us for the foreseeable future. Investments that protect purchasing power are a must for the boomer whose life expectancy is close to 100.

Instant gratification usually means long-term investment failure. The investor who seeks high short-term returns will often sell at the wrong time (i.e., low) and buy at the wrong time (i.e., high). It's important to realize that every asset class and every investment fluctuates. Investors must guard against the urge to feel good instantly and all the time. For the best results over time, hang in.

Diversification reduces risk. No investment goes up all the time. The S&P 500 has gone up for 1995, 1996, and 1997 with unparalleled returns. Don't be deceived. The S&P 500 performance is not always this good. See the chart based on Ibbotson's historical records in Appendix A for the year-by-year fluctuations and annual average returns going back to 1926. Remain diversified. It increases the likelihood that one investment will go up when another is down and vice versa.

Stocks and bonds fluctuate in price. If you miss the chance to buy low, be assured there will be another opportunity as prices of all stocks and bonds go up and down. When the first news about the impotence drug, Viagra, began to leak out in the fall of 1997, for example, Pfizer's price was $85 a share. By the time the drug was announced as being available for use, it was April 1998, when the price for a share of Pfizer was $91. During the next month when Viagra was being reported in the media, Pfizer's share price jumped as high as $118 a share. After about two weeks, it was back down to $101 a share. Patient investors who didn't know to buy in the fall of 1997 could have bought in mid-April 1998 for about $100 a share and will probably be all right with a long-term view. By the time you read this book some six or seven months after it is edited for the last time, the share price could be higher, lower, or it will have split and begun to rise again. The moral is to buy when you have the money and wait for the price to grow over time. Your account will fluctuate less with mutual funds, but you will still be wise to buy and hold.

> *"An investor's worst enemy is not the stock market
> but oneself."*
>
> —*Anonymous, from* Wit and Wisdom of Wall Street

The best investors look beyond short-term fluctuations.   In May 1998 Hewlett Packard's quarterly earnings dropped below management's expectations and caused its stock price to drop $8 a share. This drop in price doesn't mean Hewlett Packard is a bad investment. It may or may not be. All the drop tells you is that its short-term performance is not too good. Look at the long term and buy based on that. Study the Ibbotson chart in Appendix A again, and you'll notice that if the stock market is down for one or two years, the next year or two are usually good ones.

Time is more important than timing in investing.   In the history of our market, the worst 20 years are better than the best 10 years. On August 25, 1987, the Dow Jones industrial average (DJIA) was at 2722. On October 19, 1987, it had fallen to 1738. It would have been bad timing if you had purchased on August 24, 1987, and wanted to sell on October 20, 1987. But in early 1998 the DJIA topped out at 9000 and over these 11 years, you would have had a very good return. Give your investments time.

Investors can make money in flat markets.   From 1968 to 1982 the Dow gained one point. In November 1968 it was at 1004 and in November 1982 at 1005. So in 14 years it made one point. And you wouldn't have made much money. But in many mutual funds, you would have tripled your money because the managers had been selecting companies that paid dividends and capital gains that would have been reinvested to buy more shares of stock that would have paid dividends. To make money in flat markets, look for mutual funds that buy stocks that pay dividends as opposed to capital gains. For example, Bank of New York has paid dividends every year since 1785, dividends that can be used to buy additional shares. By contrast, Excite and Yahoo! seek capital gains for their investors and do not pay dividends. In a flat market, a Bank of New York investor will make money; an investor in Excite or Yahoo! might or might not make money—probably not.

Successful investors understand the benefits of time.   A mere $100 a month at 10 percent will grow to $226,049 over 30 years. Over 10 years, at 10 percent the same $100 a month will grow to $20,485.

Historically, dividends from a portfolio of successful companies rise over the long term.   As companies grow they become more valuable. When they become more valuable, they make more money. When they make more money, they can pay out more dividends to shareholders.

Selling at the bottom and buying at the top is natural for most people. Why? Most of us gravitate to what has done well lately. The bigger the number, the more I'm interested. The smaller the number, the less I'm interested because we all have an aversion to smaller numbers. We tend to want to invest in the last good experience we had instead of looking for the next good experience. The solution is to buy a variety of mutual funds. Buy some with small-cap companies, some with medium-size companies, some with large, blue chip companies, and some with international companies.

Patience is an investor's most valuable asset.

—*Anonymous*

Words for the Wise Investor

- Devise a tax strategy: Investments may be chosen so that you (1) never pay taxes (best), (2) pay in the future (next best), or (3) pay taxes annually (worst).

   1. Through Roth IRAs and life insurance products, investment interest, dividends, and capital gains may be reinvested and withdrawn with no tax liability under current tax laws and if structured properly (never pay).

   2. Taxes are paid in the future on the dollars you invested and deducted and on the gains earned through qualified plans such as individual retirement accounts (IRAs), 401(k)s, pension or profit-sharing plans, and insurance company annuities (pay in the future).

3. Examples of investments subject to annual taxes are interest-bearing alternatives primarily purchased through banks, and dividend and short-term and long-term gain income on stocks, bonds, and mutual funds commonly purchased through a brokerage firm.

• Hedge against inflation: Investments that protect purchasing power against inflation before and after retirement are especially essential for boomers, who well may reach the age of 100.

• Defer gratification: Resist the urge to seek short-term investment gratification; every asset class and every investment fluctuates.

• Diversify your investments: The old cliché, "Don't put all your eggs in one basket," is applicable; diversify and remain diversified. Diversification reduces risk.

• Never panic because you didn't buy low: Be assured there will be another opportunity.

• Buy on the basis of long-term performance: Long-term performance is a better indicator than short-term fluctuations.

• Be patient: Give your investments time to grow. Another cliché: Rome wasn't built in a you-know-what.

• There is money to be made in flat markets: Buy when you have the money and look for mutual funds that buy stocks paying dividends as opposed to capital gains. The dividends can be used to buy additional shares.

• Use time to your advantage: Small amounts of money invested consistently over many years produce better returns than larger amounts invested over a few years.

• Invest in funds containing stocks of successful companies: Historically, the dividends they pay rise over the long term.

• Don't succumb to investing out of familiarity: We tend to invest in the last good experience when we should look instead for the next good experience. The best way to do this is through a balanced variety of mutual funds.

Outsourced, Downsized, Reengineered

What Do You Do Now?

"The best time to start thinking about your retirement is before your boss does."

—*Anonymous, from* Phillips' Book of Great Thoughts, Funny Sayings

"I am escaped with the skin of my teeth."

—*Job 19:20*

DOWNSIZING: THE SAD TALE OF MARY LOU

She sat on the sofa in my office, noticeably fidgety, her face flushed. She seemed to have a hard time concentrating on our conversation. She said she had a pounding headache. Mary Lou, a 48-year-old boomer, was being shown the door by the company where she had worked for 30 years. Her world was dissolving before her eyes.

She was filled with anxiety and questions with no answers. Where was the justice in what the company was doing to her? What about loyalty? What about being "part of the team"? Her performance evaluations were always the highest, and she had survived two previous downsizings because, she had been told, she was "such a valued employee." Now she was being thrown away like an old shoe, asked to leave a job and friends she loved.

Suddenly the work ethic on which she had long relied had gone up in smoke. She had prided herself on doing her job well. Do your best, stick to the job until it is done, and the rewards will come, her parents had taught her. Yet her faithful performance of duty had not been enough.

> *"Every tub must stand on its own bottom."*
>
> —*Anonymous, from* Phillips' Book of Great Thoughts,
> Funny Sayings

Pollan and Levine noted in *Surviving the Squeeze* that until recently, people assumed that if they worked hard, their employers would take care of them. Blue-collar workers might get laid off when business slowed down, but would be rehired when business picked up. White-collar workers thought the only reason they would be terminated would be for doing something wrong. . . . These illusions were painfully shattered beginning in the late 1980s.

The simple truth is that those old assumptions no longer hold true. Today, our reliance must be on ourselves, on the skills and the inventiveness we bring to whatever work we do.

Mary Lou is just one of the many boomers who come to my office almost every day after having been downsized, outsourced, reengineered—that is, "let go." In the midst of their fright, they must pick up the pieces and evaluate them. They must assess their marketable skills and how they can be used in a different arena or in one similar to the one they are leaving. They must assess their financial situation and goals. They must make a plan, implement it, and stick to it.

In this chapter we'll look at some of the steps to getting back on your feet after you've been let go and some of the actual case histories of people who've been through it, survived it, and in many cases thrived. We'll begin with Mary Lou and her husband John.

Solutions for Mary Lou and John

John.   When Mary Lou came to my office as a downsized "valuable employee," she wasn't a stranger to me. She and her husband, John, had first been here three years before when John had been let go.

Also a 48-year-old boomer, John had been employed by a large retail establishment since he was 18 and had worked his way up to head of the maintenance staff. But in spite of his faithful service, John was asked to leave and offered a pension lump sum that seemed shockingly small for a 26-year employee: $62,000. Fortunately, John had saved for many years in the company's 401(k) plan and had accumulated $88,476 there, making the total he had to invest for retirement $150,476.

Together, Mary Lou, John, and I made a plan. John would work seven more years and let his retirement funds grow, and Mary Lou would continue to work. John felt that because he had begun working so young, he would be ready to retire at 55.

The past three years had worked out fine for John. He started his own building maintenance business and landed a contract that his former employer had let lapse when John left: maintenance work for the city. John had pursued the contract with a vengeance; it was a natural for him because he had performed the same service as an employee. Now he was the boss.

John's business thrived. He added clients, and his income was more than it would have been had he stayed with his former employer. John's investments also thrived. In three years his original investment in mutual funds of $150,476 had grown to $255,498. He had put his money into the funds at a good time and he earned 19.3 percent a year each year. According to plan, he had been able to live on the earnings from his business and his wife's salary, never touching his retirement dollars.

John had been under a lot of stress throughout the three years after he was downsized. He was afraid he wouldn't make it, but he had made it very well. Still, the stress and uncertainty of launching himself alone had taken its toll on his health. Toward the end of his third year, John experienced pain that signaled heart trouble and resulted in angioplasty. By the time Mary Lou came to my office with news that she had lost her job, John was recovering well but had slowed down his pace a bit.

Mary Lou.   Mary Lou had not thought losing her job could happen to her. She had been asked to leave the only employer she ever had a good five years before she had planned to, and the loss of her job affected other areas of her life. The extra dollars her income provided were helping their son, who had just married, and their daughter, Anna, who had just finished college. Anna, who has severe medical problems, partici-pated in Mary Lou's company's health insurance as a dependent. Now, that insurance would not be available to her.

Mary Lou's mom lived in Florida alone, had just broken her hip, and needed around-the-clock help that her Social Security income wouldn't cover. Mary Lou had thought she could help. Now she wasn't sure.

It was all too much for Mary Lou that day in my office. After a quick review of how John's investments had performed and a brief look at alter-native recommendations for placing her dollars, she graciously apologized and said she had an excruciating headache, so bad she was nauseated. She asked John to drive her home.

Mary Lou, two weeks later.   Mary Lou came back to my office two weeks later. She was still scared, but she had been to her chiropractor four times and gotten rid of her headache. We made plans for her money to be invested when it was available, and she told me her coworkers had planned a retirement party for her. Before she was to leave the company in two months, she was going to take a one-week vacation immediately to stay with her mom.

Things were looking up for Mom. Mary Lou's sister had found a nurse to stay with her for a reasonable hourly wage, and Mom was enrolled with an alarm beeper for night emergencies.

Mary Lou, two months later.   Two months after Mary Lou's world seemed on the verge of dissolution, some good news came. Anna, who had begun looking for a job, found one with low pay but great health benefits. It would begin as soon as she graduated.

At Mary Lou's office, her countdown to unemployment was over. She cleared her desk and got through the retirement party.

Mary Lou, one year later.   One year after her employment was termi-nated, Mary Lou came into my office a changed woman. She was all smiles. "I can't believe it," she said. "I haven't missed my company at all. I've been so busy. I went to Florida a lot during the year and Mom is okay. Anna got a job and has done well. John's business is flourishing, even at his slower pace. We've changed our lifestyle. We've been eating differ-ently and exercising. We've both lost 15 pounds and feel so much bet-ter!" There was, Mary Lou had found, life after downsizing.

Like John's investments, Mary Lou's were doing well. Their life was going in a different direction but going well. They had turned the corner.

Analysis.   Mary Lou and John are now doing well but it didn't happen overnight. In fact, they had saved for many years and had done some planning for retirement ahead of time, perhaps without even realizing it. Now, they are seeing the results of that planning and benefiting from it immeasurably.

> *"Chop your own wood, and it will warm you twice."*
>
> —*Henry Ford, Sr.*

OPTIONS IF YOU'RE KICKED OUT

Losing a job to downsizing, outsourcing, or reengineering is always stressful. The amount of stress, however, depends on the circumstances.

- Young people who are downsized but have a transferable skill experience the least stress. They usually see the life change as an opportunity.
- People who remain working for their companies through a vendor that is contracting their services (i.e., outsourced) experience stress that is a bit more than minimal but still tolerable. They are initially stressed out by the unknown. When they see that they still have a job, perhaps at the same work station, and the only difference is the issuer of their paycheck, they relax considerably. Then when their vendor finds them a better assignment and they make a change, it becomes obvious to them that being outsourced turned into an opportunity.
- People who are downsized or reengineered and have no skills except those of a middle manager and no alternative job readily available experience the most stress. For them it is out the roof!

Three kinds of options face those in one of these groups:

1. Career options
2. Financial options
3. Attitude options

Career Options

*"Whenever you see a successful business, someone
once made a courageous decision."*

—*Peter Drucker*

Because career options are the ones that provide bread-and-butter money, they typically are the ones that create the most stress. In my role as a financial counselor, I often find myself helping with the personal stress side of the coin first. This seems to be necessary before a client can deal rationally with the financial options.

In my office I have seen people whose jobs have been eliminated cope with reality in many ways. Some react more drastically than others, and such reactions are understandable. The stress of not having a job after having had one for so many years is highly disorienting. The knowledge that income is needed but not available to support yourself or your family leads to feelings of despair. Yet, although we have seen many people in these circumstances, not a single one has experienced the eventualities they may fear. Not a single one has committed suicide, gone bankrupt, gotten a divorce, or become homeless. Always they have found a way to go on.

Many among the hundreds of people I have worked with over the past 18 years have found new career pathways after they were downsized. In general, new career pathways may include

- starting your own similar business or one in another field in which you are skilled;
- becoming a self-employed freelance contractor, even contracting back to your old company;
- signing up with a temporary service;
- going back to school and beginning on a completely different career path; or
- working as an employee for another company in a capacity similar to the one you left.

Among my clients who have found lower-level jobs unrelated to those they left have been those who ended up working at large companies such as Home Depot, Sam's Club, Wal-Mart, KPMG/Peat Marwick, and

Kroger. At Home Depot, one woman is working in gardening, one man in hardware.

At Sam's Club, three former telephone company linemen, who were friends at work for many years, now call themselves the Three Musketeers and help open new stores and do food tastings. One man works in the produce department at Kroger and another is a management consultant on Year 2000 projects at KPMG/Peat Marwick.

Others have ventured into completely different but specialized fields for which they had an affinity or skills (or in some cases went back to school to acquire the skills). These have included assisting a pharmacist, appraising or selling real estate, bookkeeping, accounting, consulting, editing, newspaper reporting, financial planning, maintaining greens at a golf course, running a pressure-washing business, subcontracting electrical work, building homes, constructing storage buildings and carports, desktop publishing, contracting with companies to provide part-time help with computer technology, training workers in technical skills, selling antiques, selling and/or making arts and crafts, making cabinets, providing home care for the elderly, and providing child care.

Some downsized employees chose to go to work for small companies, where, using the skills they had acquired at large companies, they helped grow the fledgling businesses. Some of these formerly "let go" people are reaping big financial rewards after the small companies they helped to build went public or after they were bought out by a larger company or partner.

Financial Options

Since we are talking here about people being forced out of their jobs earlier than they had planned, the financial options are limited to "variations on a theme." These are people who had planned to work 10 to 15 more years and, as a rule, hadn't given much thought to their retirement finances. They had either invested for retirement or not—but, whichever the case, had not given it much thought!

Their financial options are the following:

- *Work full-time at the same or higher pay*. The first option is to find another job earning roughly the same or more income and, as originally planned, continue working for another 10 to 15 years and continue to save toward retirement at 65 or earlier if possible. Often, this is the case with someone who is outsourced.

- *Work either part-time or full-time while earning less than in the former job.* The second option is to work at a lesser-paying job, either part-time or full-time depending on your skills and their marketability in today's world. This option may require you to withdraw some income from retirement savings. Sometimes, a career burnout is the flip side of this alternative; that is, some don't want to work full-time even if they can earn the income they need. The financial option of withdrawing income from retirement funds early is often the solution, even if not the one to be approached quickly as it will hinder investment growth and possibly mean you'll have to work part-time longer; but sometimes, it is the only option.

- *Don't work at all.* The third option is to not work at all. Major career burnout, failing health, the failing health of parents, or fear of their own failing health in the near future often pushes people to retire earlier than they had originally planned.

- *Significantly reduce your living costs and either work or withdraw income from investments and not work.* As soon as you learn that you will lose your job, practice living on less income. The fourth option is to withdraw income that is sufficient to meet a lowered cost of living without working at all. Or some are willing to work at a much lower income in order to do "what they have always wanted to do!" More and more people coming into my office have decided to move to smaller homes, either in the same city or in a retirement community, with the goal of reducing their cost of living and "simplifying their lives." Others have simple lifestyles already and are in a position to pay off their home mortgage so as to immediately reduce their cost of living substantially.

CASE IN POINT

Choosing a Financial Option
(Kenny and Sherry)

*K*enny and Sherry, now 50-year-old boomers, are natives of New Orleans, and even though they have lived in Atlanta for 14 years, they still have soft southern Louisiana accents. When Kenny and Sherry say the word "house," it has an "oo" in it.

Two days after Kenny graduated from high school 32 years ago, he went to work for a large Fortune 500 utility company in New Orleans, and three months later, he married his high school sweetheart, Sherry. They were both 18. When Sherry and Kenny were 34 years old, he took a job in Atlanta with a different but related, Fortune 500 company and worked there 14 years until he was 48.

Kenny had planned to work until he was 55, but the company kept offering him retirement packages that got sweeter and sweeter. He was tempted but was determined to work at least a total of 30 years with the two companies, at which time his health benefits would extend into his retirement years at no cost to him. Finally, two days before the 30-year anniversary, Kenny took a retirement package, and his boss let him work a bonus two days to secure the health benefits.

At the time of his retirement, Kenny was making a base pay of $42,000 and as much as $54,000 with overtime. Now his company was about to pay him a pension of $13,200 a year. He and Sherry couldn't make it on that income alone, of course, and they wondered what they should do. They came to see me.

Kenny had a 401(k) worth $86,000, but he didn't want to touch that because he would have to pay the 10 percent early withdrawal penalty. I told him there was another way. Under the Internal Revenue Code, section 72(t), he could withdraw income penalty-free as long as he took substantially equal withdrawals at a reasonable interest rate over his life expectancy and didn't change the withdrawals for five years or until age 59½, whichever happened last. (See the Internal Revenue Code section summary containing these rules in Appendix C.)

After thinking for a couple of weeks, Kenny and Sherry chose not to withdraw income from retirement funds but chose to let them grow. Kenny was still young at 48, and he decided to continue working enough to supplement the pension. The couple used $19,000 of his severance pay, which he could not roll over, to pay off the mortgage on their house, thus reducing their already modest cost of living.

For a month, Kenny didn't work, but "he is an active person," Sherry said, "and he needed to stay busy." Then, as if it were preordained, he found the perfect job: a greenskeeper at a country club. He had always been an outdoors person who had to work indoors. Now he was an outdoors person working where he wanted to work—outside!

As a greenskeeper, Kenny would earn about $14,000 a year (with raises each year). Added to his pension of $13,200, he could cover his and Sherry's $24,000-a-year after-tax cost of living (we estimate they will owe about $2,000 in taxes) without her having to go to work.

Now that Sherry and Kenny knew they wouldn't have to withdraw income from their retirement nest egg, they wanted to invest their 401(k) money in a moderately conservative way so that by age 62 Kenny wouldn't have to work if he didn't want to.

We decided to invest his 401(k) $86,000 in mutual funds whose performance since 1973 has averaged 13 percent a year and are managed by a team of managers. Kenny also held a variety of company stocks totaling $35,000, which we expected would grow at least 10 percent a year. By age 62, if he decided not to work, Kenny could replace his greenskeeper income through a combination of Social Security dollars and income from his investments.

Two years later. Two years after Kenny took his retirement package and went to work outdoors, his and Sherry's investments looked like this:

Asset	Original Amount	Growth Amount
401(k)	$ 86,000	$125,351
Stocks	$ 35,000	$ 45,486
Total	$121,000	$170,837

In two years' time, the 401(k) money that was invested in mutual funds managed by the American Funds group and diversified among U.S. and non-U.S. small, medium, and large companies and had grown 20.73 percent a year net of all fees, and Kenny's telephone stocks had grown 14 percent a year. (Granted, these two years, 1996 and 1997, had been exceptional ones.)

Kenny is happy. He gets time off from his less demanding job to go hunting and fishing, and his blood pressure, high when he worked indoors, has gone down of its own accord. "He'll probably work there until he is so old he can't walk," Sherry chuckled. "The people at the club love him because he's older and responsible."

Sherry is happy too. She keeps the grandchildren a day or two a week. She and Kenny both cook the Cajun food they love and indulge in their one luxury: vacations. "We like to go places," she said, "but we don't blow money."

A look at Kenny and Sherry's future. How much in future dollars will Kenny and Sherry need at age 62 to support their $24,000 cost of living if inflation continues to average 3 percent a year?

To be able to spend in 14 years the same amount of money they are spending today, they will need $36,302 after taxes, which means they will need about $39,000 before taxes.

Kenny found out from the Social Security Administration that his expected income at age 62 will be $835 a month, or $10,020 a year. Here's the analysis of his retirement income needs at that time.

Income needed	$ 39,000
Less Social Security	(10,020)
Less pension*	(13,200)
Income shortfall	($ 15,780)
Retirement nest egg needed	$225,428
Current nest egg	$170,837
14-year growth needed	2% a year

*Assume the pension does not increase.

Wrap-up. The growth the couple needs is entirely achievable. Even if they have to move from stocks, where the expected return ranges from 10 to 12 percent a year, they can reasonably expect to earn 5 to 8 percent in bonds. In fact, they would earn the needed return with no risk in T-bills or insured savings deposits.

Kenny and Sherry literally began on a wing and a prayer. They had a small amount to start with, and they knew he may have to work till 65. That was okay with them.

After all, they never expected to be millionaires. They had created a lifestyle that didn't demand a million dollars. But they feel good about where they are. They own a home with no mortgage that they had bought 22 years ago for $103,000. Today it is worth $130,000. Both cars are paid for, and they have no other debt.

"Things" don't mean a lot to them. Family is what matters. Kenny and Sherry have sent both of their children to see me so they can start investing early. They realize they probably should have saved more along the way and started earlier. But the main thing is that they are happy. Their financial security is assured because they are happy with a modest lifestyle.

Kenny and Sherry's options with no pension.   Because pensions are gone for future generations, let's look at Kenny and Sherry's numbers above to see where they would have been if there had been no pension. Future generations will have to rely on their own retirement savings. Therefore, it will be more imperative to begin investing early and at the maximum amount allowed by your tax-deferred plan.

Option 1: When Kenny lost his $54,000-a-year job, he could have found another job earning $26,000 a year that would represent income to cover the couple's cost of living, including taxes. Gone would be Kenny's dreams of working on the golf course unless Sherry could find work paying $12,000 a year.

Option 2: The couple could have kept their cost of living the same. If they did, they could supplement Kenny's golf club income ($14,000 a year) with income from their retirement funds ($9,000 a year) and Sherry would have had to find a job ($3,000 a year).

Option 3: They could have reduced their cost of living by $3,000 a year so Sherry wouldn't have to work. To withdraw adequate income from Kenny's retirement funds, it would mean that he would be withdrawing 8 percent a year, leaving only 3 to 4 percent for growth.

If they had selected the second option, in 14 years at 3 percent inflation, their inflated cost of living would be about $39,000. Let's see if they could make it under this scenario:

Income needed	$ 39,000
Less Social Security	($ 10,020)
Income shortfall	$ 28,980
Retirement nest egg needed	$414,000
Current nest egg	$170,837
14-year growth needed	6.5% a year

Even under the scenario above, in which Kenny gets no pension money, the investment growth the couple would need is possible. As in the previous example, moving to a much more conservative option would still provide the growth they need. They could invest in bonds and expect to receive about 5 to 8 percent a year.

It would be good if they could average 12 percent a year for the first few years; so it will be important to keep a close watch on their asset positioning—especially early in the investment growth years.

As a final fallback position, they could work until age 65, when Kenny's retirement nest egg would have grown larger and his Social Security income would be more.

SUGGESTIONS FOR COPING FINANCIALLY

"Waste not, want not."

—Benjamin Franklin

Consider downsizing your existing home.   If the kids are gone, you may be smarter to find a smaller home. The new tax laws now allow us to take the capital gain from our homes tax-free and buy a smaller home. This is a good time to buy that home you plan to live in until retirement.

Keep your cars longer and when you buy, don't buy new. Make those cars last at least seven years. If you've paid for them over three or four years, you'll have some years to save what was your payment toward the down payment for your next car, thus decreasing the payment in the future.

Stop taking expensive trips.   Use your frequent flyer miles, of course, but don't forget to visit relatives and friends for a night or two along the way. It will help cement those relationships you've had to ignore for those busy child-rearing years and it will be cost-effective, too. As for overseas travel, remember that there are many places in this country you can see by car for a lot less money. Figure out how to create memories with your family that are less expensive.

Stop going to the mall "just to look" because it never turns out to be just a sight-seeing trip. Go shopping only when you need something; shop for that particular thing and leave.

Reduce your gift-buying budget. Buy gifts during the year that you can use for weddings. Develop your Christmas list in January and catch sales during the year.

Stay with growth investments until you need to start withdrawing income. Growth investments translate to aggressive investing, meaning you'll want to own mutual funds that invest in companies that pay small or no dividends. These are companies that keep dividends inside the company to help the company grow. The stock prices of such companies tend to be volatile, so if you need income, you'll want to minimize the number of such funds in your portfolio. If you don't need income, you can afford to own some of them and use time to help you ride out the potential down cycles that do inevitably come.

Plan to work longer. By working longer, you'll be able to invest more aggressively. Furthermore, because most of us will live long lives, we'll need to keep our minds active. And working is one of the best ways to feed your mind. Remember, your brain is a muscle. It, like all the other muscles in your body, will atrophy if it isn't exercised.

Attitude Options

> *"There really are only three types of people: those who make things happen, those who watch things happen, and those who say, 'What happened?'"*
>
> —*Ann Landers*

Attitude makes a big difference in the successful transition from the warmth of a secure job to a life beyond, I've observed. Those who see their premature job loss as a positive consider it an opportunity to grow and experience something else in life. Those people usually determine from the beginning that it will work and it always does.

Those who see their job loss as a negative often feel as though they have been treated unfairly—slapped in the face by the company they loved! They frequently look for ways to get back at the company. They are the ones who seek revenge through lawsuits charging discrimination or refuse their company's offer to contract them back—effectively only hurting themselves.

CASE IN POINT

Downsized Employee Turned Motivational Speaker
(Kevin)

"Your living is determined not so much by what life brings
to you as by the attitude you bring to life."

—*John Homer Miller*

*K*evin found himself one day in a large auditorium with 600 of his fellow workers being addressed by the vice president of marketing of a large Fortune 500 company: "I have been asked to tell you that the company will be downsizing 10,000 jobs within the next six months. Our department will be affected. As a result, six months from now 80 percent of you will not be here. I am sorry to have to bring you this news."

After a few moments of complete silence as everyone sat stunned, Kevin raised his hand and was recognized: "I have just one question. After all those people are gone, can I move to a large corner office with windows?" The room burst with laughter. A man on the front row piped up: "I'm his best friend, can I have the office next to his?" But the guy sitting next to Kevin jabbed him with his elbow and said, "You dummy, you'll probably be the first to go!"

Kevin had used his sense of humor to relieve the tension of the moment. It was in that moment that he decided to be what he calls proactive and make the best of a bad situation. And I'll tell you his story. But the guy who called him a dummy is still bitter and still unemployed.

Kevin's father had worked for the same company as Kevin and had retired after 30 years. It shocked him to learn that his son was being let go after 17 years of loyal service. Kevin and his dad were close, so Kevin wanted to talk it out with him.

Kevin had decided to earn his living by becoming a motivational speaker. When he told his dad, his dad said: "What if you don't make it? You may have to sell your fancy car and buy an old clunker!" Kevin replied, "Dad, I'll do whatever it takes." Dad: "You may have to quit eating out so much." Kevin: "Dad, I'll do whatever it takes." Dad: "But, Son, you may even have to move back in with us!" Kevin: "Dad, I'll do whatever it takes." Dad finally said: "Son, I believe you're going to make it."

Today, three years later, Kevin is a successful motivational speaker and has written a book. His income is higher than it was when he left his company.

Kevin had been downsized at age 41, and had only about $60,000 in his 401(k). He wouldn't be able to draw his pension of $600 a month until age 65. His $60,000 is now invested and he and I are hoping it will earn at least 12 percent a year. At that rate, he'll have $910,000 when he's 65, assuming he doesn't invest another dime toward retirement. But he plans to invest at least $10,000 a year toward retirement from 45 to 65. He thinks his business will be mature enough then to provide the investment money he needs. Let's look at his financial picture:

Asset	*Projected to Age 65**
401(k)	$ 910,000
$10,000 per year	806,987
Total	$1,716,987

*Assumes 12% a year return

The $1,716,987 will produce about $120,000 a year in income to support Kevin in retirement—the equivalent of about $60,000 a year in today's dollars. Kevin believes he can live on that income. He will be financially independent even if we ignore his $600 a month pension and Social Security income.

His attitude made all the difference!

"Attitude adjustment is a check-up from the neck-up!"

—*Zig Ziglar*

*"Instead of crying over spilt milk, go milk
another cow."*

—*Erna Asp*

Moving to the future after downsizing. If you're downsized, your attitude may not keep you from being successful financially, but it will certainly play a large part. If you choose to be negative, your entire body will display those feelings. If you accept the inevitable and adopt a positive attitude, your body will reflect that as well.

If you had a choice of being around someone who is negative or someone who is positive, which person would you choose? Your next employer or contractor will be making that choice also. Do yourself a favor; adjust your attitude.

It doesn't matter what your attitude was when you started reading this chapter; what matters is the attitude you have when you finish reading it.

*"Words can never adequately convey the incredible
impact of our attitude toward life. The longer
I live the more convinced I become that life is
10 percent what happens to us and 90 percent
how we respond to it."*

—*Charles R. Swindoll*

SUGGESTED READING

Keith D. Harrell, *Attitude Is Everything: A Tune-Up to Enhance Your Life* (Dubuque, Iowa: Kendall/Hunt Publishing Co., 1997)

Perry W. Buffington, Ph.D. (a.k.a. "Dr. Buff"), *Cheap Psychological Tricks: What to Do When Hard Work, Honesty, and Perseverance Fail* (Atlanta: Peachtree Publishers, 1996)

Sarah Ban Breathnach, *Simple Abundance: A Daybook of Comfort and Joy* (New York: Warner Books, 1995)

A Checklist for the Downsized Boomer

Following is a brief summary of ways to implement the three types of options available to downsized boomers:

1. Review your career options.

   - Start your own business.

   - Become a freelance contractor.

   - Sign with a temporary service.

   - Go back to school and prepare for a different career.

2. Review your financial options.

   - Find another full-time job at the same or better pay.

   - Work part-time or full-time at less pay than before and withdraw some from your retirement investments.

   - Retire early and don't work at all.

   - Reduce your cost of living, draw retirement income, and don't work.

3. Maintain a positive attitude.

   - Don't worry about things you can't control.

   - Don't worry about things that haven't happened.

   - Don't worry about things that really don't matter.

   - Don't take yourself too seriously.

   - Call on friends and relatives who can help you stay upbeat.

   - Find your passion.

   - Determine to do whatever it takes to make your next move a positive one.

Caring for Your Parents

A Special Issue for Boomers

"When I can't find someone in my office in Washington, it's not because a child fell down. It's because of a crisis with an aging parent."

—*U. S. Commissioner on Aging Carol Fraser Fisk*

*G*ood health care and good nutrition have created in the United States and other industrialized nations an increasingly older population the likes of which the world has never seen. By the year 2000 as much as one-fifth of our population will be over 65. Today, a woman who is 65 can expect to live to age 87 and a man who is 65 today can expect to live to age 83 according to mortality tables for nonsmokers used to compute mortality for people who may buy life insurance. The longer a person lives, the longer he or she can expect to live.

The numbers are astonishing when you look at life expectancies since our nation was formed, according to *Collier's Encyclopedia*. When the Second Continental Congress adopted the Declaration of Independence in 1776, for example, the average life expectancy at birth for women was 36.5 years and for men 34.5. Parents lived only a few years after their last child left the nest. In 1890, the average life expectancy was about 44 and less than 4 percent of the nation's population was over 65. By 1900 women could expect to live to be about 51 and men 48, and by 1956 both men and women were living on average to age 69.9. By 1985 life expectancy was about 75.

PHYSICAL AND FISCAL CARE FOR PARENTS

With today's longer life spans, boomers face the growing responsibility of seeing that their parents are well cared for physically and financially. Boomers must make sure their parents get their flu shots annually and their once-a-lifetime pneumonia shot. They often are responsible for making the routine check-up appointments for their parents and arranging the transportation for them. Encouragement for regular exercising and some social activities also fall within the scope of our concerns.

This is why many seniors do better in retirement living arrangements where an activities calendar is kept and they are encouraged to participate.

Boomer Budgets and Retirement Plans Taxed by Parents

Many of us look forward to the day we can retire early and travel, unencumbered by children. Some of us are willing to drastically change our lifestyles and live on less income just to escape the corporate rat race a few years early. But in today's world, even if children are out of the nest, our parents may be *in* the nest. In some cases, we are even supplementing the incomes of our parents in one form or another.

CASE IN POINT

Boomers Taking Responsibility for Aging Parents
(Jesse and Nell)

"Responsibility is the thing people dread most of all. Yet it is the only thing in the world that develops us, gives us manhood or womanhood fibre."

—Anonymous, from Phillip's Book of Great Thoughts, Funny Sayings

Some boomers take their parents into their own homes to physically provide a home for them. Such was the case with Jesse and Nell. Jesse's dad is fighting prostate cancer and after his mother had a nondisabling stroke, Jesse and Nell finished their basement to provide a full apartment for his parents. The recently increased costs of their medications made it impossible for the parents to continue to pay for independent housing in the apartment where they lived.

Now, Jesse, 53, has decided to take the early retirement package his company is offering. He and Nell, who is a registered nurse working part-time, would like to move to Tennessee where their son and daughter-in-law are living.

Jesse said, "This is a hard decision, because I don't want to have to uproot my parents again. Besides that, I'm afraid we won't have the money when I retire to buy another house, pay for moving all four of us, and still help my parents financially when we move. And here I am, wanting to retire and not work!"

The first issue was to find out whether his parents were up for the move if the finances could be worked out. A thorough discussion revealed they were. So Jesse and Nell came to me for help.

Jesse's parents' income is $843 a month from Social Security. They pay Jesse and Nell $343 a month for rent. They buy their own food and medicines, which are expensive. Jesse's dad is on a hormone pill that retards the growth of prostate cancer; the prescription costs about $300 a month and is not covered by Medicare. His mom takes thyroid medication and blood pressure medicine costing $100 a month. So the remaining $100 a month has to cover all other cost of living items. Some months it does and some months Jesse and Nell supplement the parents' income about an estimated $200. So from the $343 a month rent Jesse and Nell receive, on average they net about $143 a month.

Options available for Jesse and Nell.   Let's explore two options Jesse and Nell could choose for their maximum benefit as well as for his parents.

Option 1: Withdraw from rollover to cover shortfall.   I helped Jesse and Nell examine their financial options. Their son lives in a community in Tennessee where they can buy a lot of house for much less than they can in Atlanta. One option then is to buy a home in Tennessee with enough land for a manufactured home nearby for the elderly parents. Jesse and Nell could use their son's help in looking after the grandparents. Also, Nell could help take care of her granddaughter. With someone to help look after his parents, Jesse and Nell can travel some.

Their current home in Atlanta is worth $290,000, on which they have a $140,000 mortgage with $1,600-a-month payments. They could probably sell the Atlanta home, and after paying the 6 percent real estate commission of $17,400 and the mortgage, they would net $132,600.

In the small Tennessee town they estimate they could buy as much house as they want with two acres for about $120,000 cash from the equity from their home. For $20,000 they could buy a manufactured home (formerly called a mobile home) and place it on their property so Jesse's parents could still live close by but be independent. They can put $8,000 down from the home sale proceeds on the manufactured home but will still need $12,000. They were thinking about using $5,000 from their savings account and taking a withdrawal from his retirement rollover money to pay the $7,000 shortfall. Jesse and Nell currently have $9,000 in their savings account and no debt. They need to maintain the $4,000 balance in savings plus the extra $4,000 from the sale of their home to cover moving costs and emergencies.

In order to net $7,000, Jesse would have to liquidate about $10,000 from his rollover account. If they wait to withdraw from the account until they are in Tennessee, they will owe no state taxes. They would have to use a personal loan or borrow for about two months on a credit card if they chose this option as it will take about two months to get the rollover dollars placed and distributed. Here's the tax analysis:

Tax Analysis of Withdrawal from IRA Rollover

Total withdrawal from IRA	$10,000
Less federal taxes of 15%	(1,500*)

Less early withdrawal penalty of 10%   (1,000)
Net to Cover Shortfall $ 7,500

*Tennessee has no state tax.

This option has less appeal because it will cost them $2,500 in taxes and penalties.

Option 2: Secure a home equity loan to cover the shortfall.   This option would involve no taxes or penalties. The couple could take out a loan on their new home and to avoid closing costs, could take out a $15,000 home equity loan instead of a mortgage. This would net them enough money to pay for the move, decorate their new home, put up window treatments, and pay for other incidentals as well as leave their entire savings account for emergencies.

Home equity loan $15,000
Less balance on manufactured home   (12,000)
Net for Incidentals $ 3,000

This option would require a payment of only $225 and the interest is tax deductible. Jesse's parents still pay $343 a month and Jesse and Nell still expect to help them with about $200 a month on the average. So they will have $143 a month net from his parents to use to pay the $225 a month payment.

Their cost of living in Atlanta is contrasted in Figure 10.1 with the expected costs in the Tennessee mountains.

Jesse was really burned out. He wanted most of all to retire "for good" if possible. Of course, he knows that he may want to work somewhere at a less demanding job later, but for at least six months, Jesse wants off. So the question remains: if the family moves to Tennessee, can Jesse quit?

You can see from Figure 10.1 that the cost of living in a smaller community will be only 36 percent of what it is now in Atlanta. Now let's look at the couple's net worth and decide if their invested assets will provide the income they'll need in Tennessee.

FIGURE 10.1 A Comparison of Living Costs in Atlanta with Costs in Tennessee

Jesse and Nell's Cost of Living

Expense Categories	Atlanta (Monthly) Total	Tennessee (Monthly) Total
Home (Mortgage payment, insurance, tax, improvements, yard)	$ 2,200	$ 350
Utilities (gas, power, water, cable, phone)	410	180
Food (groceries, lunches at work, restaurants)	600	300
Recreation/Entertainment (vacations, clubs, concerts, etc.)	140	120
Automobile (payments, gas, repairs, etc.)	150	100
Medical (Doctor, drugs, insurance, etc.)	200	200
Donations/Gifts (charities, church, birthdays, holidays)	500	300
Savings/Investments (savings, reserves, investments, education funding)	400	0
Life insurance (personal, life, disability)	175	0
Personal necessities (hair, cosmetics, laundry, subscriptions)	100	50
Clothing (shoes, alterations, cleaning, etc.)	100	50
Depreciating assets (major purchases)	100	50
Pets (vet bills, prescriptions, grooming, etc.)	0	0
Children's/Parents' expenses (parties, medicine, etc.)	200	200
Total Monthly	$ 5,275	$ 1,900
Total Annually	$63,300	$22,800

Jesse and Nell's Net Worth

Assets

Fixed

Checking	$ 1,000	
Savings	9,000	
Certificate of deposit	4,000	
Subtotal		$ 14,000

Invested

Mutual funds	$ 4,000	
Employee stock purchase plan	14,800	
Lump sum pension	373,000	
401(k)	109,500	
Subtotal		$501,300

Use

Home	$280,000	
Personal property	120,000	
'89 Honda	4,000	
'93 Honda	8,000	
Subtotal		$412,000
Total Assets		$927,300

Liabilities

Home mortgage	($140,000)	
Net Worth (assets minus liabilities)		$787,300

Retirement Income Analysis

Cost of living needed	$ 25,200	
Estimated federal taxes*	3,780	
Total before-tax income needed	$ 28,980	

*Tennessee has no state tax

Resources Available:

Lump sum	$373,000	
401(k)	$109,500	
Total		$482,500

Growth subaccount set-aside	68,500
Income and growth subaccount	$414,000
Percentage withdrawal for income	× .07
Income to Spend	$ 28,980

The retirement income analysis indicates that Jesse can move his family to Tennessee and begin drawing income from a portion of his rollover, leaving $68,500 in a side fund for growth.

Before they made their final decision, Jesse and Nell also wanted to see if it would also be possible to stay in Atlanta if Jesse didn't work.

If they stayed in Atlanta and Jesse retired, their cost of living would be reduced some: He would not be investing $400 a month into his 401(k), he could drop his life insurance and save $175 a month, and because his income would be down, his charitable donations would drop about $200 a month. Therefore, their cost of living in Atlanta would be $54,000 a year instead of $63,300.

To support that cost of living and not work, Jesse and Nell would have to have a nest egg of $771,000. Therefore, between the two of them, Jesse and Nell would have to work and earn about $27,000 a year. Their earnings net after taxes and FICA plus $33,740 (7 percent of $482,000, his retirement nest egg) would give them enough to support their much higher cost of living in Atlanta. So they do indeed have viable options.

Wrap-up. After some thought, Jesse and Nell decided to make the move to Tennessee. Jesse had decided to take the early retirement stream of income under the Internal Revenue Code section 72(t) provision that allows penalty-free withdrawals from IRA accounts if the payments represent substantially equal withdrawals over the lifetime of the account holder at a reasonable interest rate and they are not changed for five years or until age 59½, whichever happens last. Certainly from a financial perspective, this is the best alternative. And in the small Tennessee town, Jesse may find a job he will enjoy. If he does and makes enough so that he doesn't need the rollover income, his monthly payments can be redirected to his mutual fund but placed into a nonqualified account (that is, outside the IRA and after taxes) with no fee for reinvestment and no penalty for withdrawal.

CASE IN POINT

A Boomer Taking Care of Mom
(David and Julie)

*D*avid, 53, and Julie, 54, make a home for her 93-year-old mom, Ruth. Ruth has lived with them since her husband died five years ago. Julie is a very productive self-employed business consultant and normally works out of her home. Until they moved to Atlanta two years ago, Ruth was fairly independent and Julie was able to work effectively out of her home. However, after her mom's almost fatal last bout with flu and an extended hospital visit, Ruth panics if Julie is out of her line of vision and begins calling her until Julie responds. Working at home is now impossible for Julie. She is her mom's full-time caregiver.

David and Julie last year sacrificed Julie's income as she was getting the family settled in a new home. This year, Julie will only earn about $20,000. In previous years, Julie's income averaged about $80,000 a year. These are the important years for them to invest for retirement and they were planning to invest all of Julie's income.

They came to see me for help in deciding how to manage their retirement savings given the fact that Julie will have little income for the foreseeable future so that she can take care of her mom. They have decided that moving her mom into an assisted living community is not a choice they will use. Here is their net worth.

David and Julie's Net Worth

Assets

Fixed Assets

Checking	$ 3,000	
Savings	22,000	
Savings bonds	5,000	
Subtotal		$30,000

Invested Assets

Mutual funds	$ 12,000
IRA rollover (Julie)	92,000
IRA rollover (David)	201,000

Deferred income (David)*	206,700	
401(k) (David)	16,800	
Stock options (David)	14,000	
Subtotal		$ 542,500

Use Assets

Home	$630,000	
Personal property	$250,000	
'97 Jaguar	$ 60,000	
'95 Jaguar	$ 45,000	
Subtotal		$ 985,000
Total Assets		$1,557,500

Liabilities

Home mortgage	($450,000)	
Car loan ('97 Jaguar)	(30,000)	
Accrued taxes on deferred income**	(62,800)	
Total Liabilities		($542,800)
Net Worth (assets less liabilities)		**$1,014,700**

*Future value of $15,000 a year @ 12% a year for 10 years beginning at age 65 is $294,800. I calculate the value of that income in today's dollars adjusted for 3% a year inflation that has a present value of $206,700.

**At the time the income is paid, taxes will be owed on the income. Therefore, note the taxes due as a liability, although they are not due now.

David has just changed jobs and earns $150,000 a year. He is looking forward to at least 12 years with the company. He will elect to defer income each year for as long as the program lasts. The deferred income will begin paying him at age 65 and each deferral can be structured annually to meet his planning for income in the future. He will receive stock options each year that will be immediately vested. He will have to wait three years before he can exercise his options but all options must be exercised within ten years of receipt, and if he leaves the company, he will have one year to exercise them. He also plans to contribute the approximate maximum of $10,000 to the 401(k) annually. Let's take a look at their retirement income analysis at their retirement date in ten years.

Retirement Income Analysis for David and Julie

Income Needed

Annual after-tax budget if retired today	$ 99,600
Annual after-tax budget if retired in 10 years	
(Inflated at 3% for 10 years)	$133,800
Taxes (estimated at 12% average)	17,827
Total Retirement Income Need	$151,627

Income Sources

Invested Assets	Current Value	Future Value*
IRAs (David)	$216,300 grown 10 yrs. @ 12%	$ 671,795
IRA (Julie)	$25,000 grown 10 yrs. @ 12%	77,600
Fixed annuity		
(Julie)	$18,000 grown 10 yrs. @ 6%	32,200
401(k) (David)	$116,600 grown 10 yrs. @ 12%	362,200
401(k) cont'd.		
(David)	$833/mo grown 10 yrs. @ 12%	193,500
Deferred income		
(David)	$1,900/mo grown 10 yrs. @ 10%	392,400
Income Account		$1,729,695
Withdrawal Percentage		× .07
Investment Income Available in Future Dollars		$121,079

In order for Julie and David to maintain their style of living, including their expensive home and cars, they will need in ten years an additional amount of retirement capital of $436,400 to produce the additional $30,548 annual income they will need. They will need to invest about $20,000 a year more to meet their goal. David is now receiving stock options and expects to for as long as he works for the company. He believes those options will be enough to cover his shortfall. If they are of no value ten years out, he will have to work about three more years to reach his financial goals.

CASE IN POINT

A Single Boomer Daughter Caring for Mom
(Donna)

"Responsibilities gravitate to the person who can shoulder them."

—*Elbert Hubbard*

*D*onna is 49 and single. She is taking the early retirement package her company is offering, but she can't afford to retire for good. She will be contracting back to her company, and because the work will involve a lot of travel, she can live almost anywhere near a major airport.

Donna has a sister and brother, but everyone expects Donna to take care of Mom. While Donna is concerned about the care of her mom, she is ultimately worried about maintaining herself in a retirement or semiretired mode. Take a look at her retirement income analysis.

Donna's Semiretirement Income Analysis

Income Needed

Annual after-tax budget if retired today	$38,028
Federal and State Taxes	11,100
FICA*	6,732
Total Retirement Income Need	**$55,860**

*Donna plans to work; therefore, she will owe FICA taxes on her earned income. When not working, she will owe no FICA.

Income Sources

Noncash Assets	*Current Value*	*Future Value*
Lump sum pension	$165,000	$165,000
401(k)	160,000	160,000
Mutual fund	2,400	2,400
Total retirement nest egg		$327,400
Growth account set-aside for future		($127,400)
Income-producing account		$200,000

Withdrawal percentage	× .07
Investment income	$ 14,000
Donna's projected earnings at new job	44,000
Total Income	**$ 58,000**

Donna knows she has to continue working. She also is the only child willing to take care of her 79-year-old Mom, who is living on a survivor's pension from her husband's former employer (the railroad) and the interest from some CDs. Because she is on a railroad pension, Mom doesn't receive Social Security. Her home is paid for but is becoming increasingly difficult for her to maintain.

Donna anticipates the home will sell for about $60,000. Added to her $40,000 CD, it can generate about $7,000 a year income from the assets; and with her railroad pension of $700 a month, she will have $15,400 a year. The assisted living community in her town charges $1,500 a month. Donna plans to let her spend down her principal until she qualifies for Medicaid. Donna thinks her mother's medicines and her personal necessities will cost about $200 a month. Her $100,000 should last about 10 to 12 years considering increasing costs over the years. Donna believes this will be enough to last for her mom's lifetime. But Donna not only has to manage the financial affairs of her mom, she has to manage the emotional concerns.

Donna's mom wants her to move back to Charlotte and buy a house the two of them can share. The finances would work out well for both of them.

"For a while, I thought about it," said Donna, "and even took a week's vacation to stay with her the entire time. But after about three days it became apparent that if I did what my mom wants, I will become a slave to her. She became more and more dependent on me every day. It didn't take long for me to realize I would be unable to work and take care of myself if my mom and I lived together . . . as much as I wish we could."

While living with her mom might be better financially, emotionally it would not. Financial decisions always involve an emotional component and this is especially true when it comes to caring for our aging parents.

CASE IN POINT

Sandwiched between Two Generations
(Norma and Walt)

*N*orma, 45, and Walt, 50, have spent three weekends helping her mom pack up and deliver the contents of her flea market business to an auction house. They had finally talked her into giving up the business she had shared with her husband of 52 years before he died last year. Norma's mom had both knees replaced several years ago and now cataract surgery is on the calendar. Norma had researched the doctors for the knee surgeries, taken her to the appointments, and will now do the same for the eye surgery. In addition, Norma is helping her husband run his printing business and is taking care of their 6-year-old son, Derek, who is playing soccer, T-ball, singing in the choir, and being generally active with his friends.

Norma's attention to her mom and to Derek is causing her to cut back her hours in the business. Walt will have to hire someone to fill Norma's position for an undetermined time. They had started their family late after many hours and dollars were invested in infertility treatments.

Assessing if Norma can afford not to work full-time.   The compromises of time and money are at work here. If the couple are willing to continue to pay for after-school care for Derek and one of Norma's brothers would help with her mom, Norma could work full-time. But Derek is of the age that they would like for Norma to be an at-home mom, and it is obvious that Norma is the only one to spend time attending to her mom's needs. So they asked me to help them evaluate the financial aspect of their goal.

This couple has decided to perform more of their household chores themselves to save the cost of lawn maintenance, house cleaning, painting, redecorating, and general fix-up. Norma plans to cook more to save money on eating out. Her income is being reduced from $35,000 a year to $15,000. Because of the loss of her income, their charitable contributions will be reduced by $200 a month. She will only have the benefit of the 15 percent contribution of her $15,000 salary (instead of her larger $35,000 salary) to the company-funded profit-sharing plan, thereby losing approximately $167 per month in retirement contributions. They will no longer be paying for after-school care for Derek, saving them $300 a month. Look at their cost of living.

Walt and Norma's Cost of Living

Expense Categories	Norma Working Monthly Total	Norma Not Working Monthly Total
Home	$ 1,230	$ 1,080
(Mortgage payment, insurance, tax, improvements, yard)		
Utilities	250	250
(gas, power, water, cable, phone)		
Food	500	300
(groceries, lunches at work, restaurants)		
Recreation/Entertainment	200	200
(vacations, clubs, concerts, etc.)		
Automobile	150	150
(payments, gas, repairs, etc.)		
Medical	200	200
(Doctor, drugs, insurance, etc.)		
Donations/Gifts	600	400
(charities, church, birthdays, holidays)		
Savings/Investments	1,125	958
(savings, reserves, investments, education funding)		
Life insurance	150	150
(personal, life, disability)		
Personal necessities	100	75
(hair, cosmetics, laundry, subscriptions)		
Clothing	250	200
(shoes, alterations, cleaning, etc.)		
Depreciating assets	100	100
(major purchases)		

Pets	50	50
(vet. bills, prescriptions, grooming, etc.)		
Children's/Parents' expenses	500	150
(parties, medicines, etc.)		
Total Monthly	$ 5,405	$ 4,263
Total Annually	$64,860	$51,156

Cost of living expenses saved	$13,740
Retirement savings not funded	2,004
Taxes saved if Norma works less	8,328
Total dollars saved by Norma working less	$24,072

They will not be paying about $6,792 a year to the IRS and the state for the income Norma won't be earning. In addition, she won't have to pay FICA on her lost $20,000 income, which will save them $1,530 a year. And she won't be contributing as much to the retirement savings program, which will save them $2,004 a year. So they will save some money by Norma's not working. They do plan for Walt to increase his gross income by $10,000 a year to help make up for Norma's lost retirement contribution as soon as his business will allow the increase. Fortunately, Norma's mom doesn't need financial help at this time.

Walt and Norma's plan.   This boomer couple is a perfect example of the squeeze many feel from parents, career, and young children. However, because they started their family late, they have made headway on reducing their mortgage to $67,633. When they began, their mortgage was $120,000 financed over 30 years at an 8 percent fixed rate. They purchased their home 21 years ago for $132,000 with a 10 percent down payment; the home is now worth $225,000. They have made no additional principal payments through the years and will have it paid for in nine more years.

Walt and Norma had begun a college fund for Derek when he was born and they continue to fund it with $150 a month. It now has $18,000 in it. Derek's aunt has an education fund for him as well with about $5,000 in it and she is continuing to fund it with $50 a month. So Derek's education will be handled.

When Derek starts college in 12 years, Walt will be 62. He is planning to retire then.

Taking care of our parents' physical needs is something we want to do. But it sometimes comes at quite a price. After all, boomers are in the middle of the prime of their lives. Careers are frantic and stressful. Children are active and demanding. We try to provide support for our spouses and we try to find time for ourselves so we won't burn out under all this stress. Then, if our parents need attention or financial support, we have yet another stress with which to deal.

CASE IN POINT

A Single Boomer Son Caring for His Mother
(John)

*W*hen John's father died five years ago, he was the sibling designated to help his mother, Jean, then 67 years of age, with her finances. This was to prove a problem because Jean, who had always depended on her husband to take care of matters pertaining to money, resisted John's efforts to manage her assets so that they would grow. "She said she won't be around long enough to need more money," John said, "but the average life expectancy is increasing. She is only 69. She may live many more years and she will need money for taxes, cars, food, medicine, and doctors. And every year the costs of those things go up. She couldn't or didn't want to understand that."

Jean had one simple desire where money was concerned. "She wanted to be able to write checks and not worry about where the money would come from," John said. "She just wanted to use what was in the pot." It was familiar ground because it was all she had ever done. Jean didn't understand two basic principles of money management in retirement: *You must protect your principal and you must protect your purchasing power.*

First, with regard to principal, there was plenty in the pot. Jean's husband had worked for the same large company for 40 years and she received his ample pension of $2,300 a month and also his Social Security income of $600 a month. But there was more; more

than Jean even realized. Her husband had put some funds into certificates of deposit (CDs) at the bank and some into IRAs in CDs.
Additionally, in the course of working, her husband had accumulated a few shares in Coca-Cola and quite a number of shares of
stock in utilities companies. The first thing John did, over the strong
protests of his mother, was to take her to a financial adviser who
switched the stocks into her name only.

John and his mother live in different states, but when he visited
her during the first two years he would review the stocks. They
were growing, but he knew they were at more risk than necessary
because they all were in a single market segment. "It was as if you
had all your money in oil," he said. "Shares of Texaco, Exxon, and
British Petroleum. What if all the oil stocks go bust? I thought she
needed to diversify. But my father hadn't diversified. She said if it
was good enough for him, it was good enough for her. She couldn't
see that the investment world is different today from the one in
which my father accumulated and held those stocks."

As an attempt to pacify John, Jean reluctantly put one of the
rollover IRA accounts with a large major brokerage firm. "But they
were always calling her," John said. "They wanted her to do this or
that with the money. This bothered her. She was leery of them. My
father always said these people are just out to make commissions.
They churn the account to make money." Although John wasn't
generally leery of all brokerage firms, he wasn't happy about the
calls, and he persuaded her to move the money to a discount brokerage firm where no one would call her.

John knew that other adjustments needed to be made that the
discount brokerage firm would not be equipped to handle. So he
persuaded Jean to go to a financial planner. With the help of this
planner, with whom she has remained, her assets were diversified
into mutual funds.

One of John's objectives was to protect the assets upon his
mom's death. A trust was established so that at her death the estate
would not have to go through probate court. "If it goes to probate,"
John said, "it goes on record in the courthouse and people can go
there and look at the record and call you. It's like when you have a
baby. People read the announcement and want to sell you things.
The vultures come out."

Jean's financial planner also referred her to an attorney who could help her make out a will and establish a medical power of attorney. Without a will that would, if structured correctly, allow her to protect $625,000 (and more between 1998 and 2006; see the estate tax rates in Appendix D) from estate taxes at her death. Her financial planner showed her that her total net worth was over $1 million and that $1 million less the $625,000 exemption (about $375,000) would be subject to federal estate taxes at about 34 percent. (See estate tax table in Appendix D.) With the help of the attorney and the financial planner, Jean learned about charitable remainder trusts, irrevocable trusts, and lifetime gifting programs to children.

Next Jean learned the value of a medical power of attorney. She assigned to John her medical power of attorney in a document that the attorney prepared. If she is incapacitated and in the hospital, John will have her permission to make decisions about her medical care after receiving the opinions of three medical professionals.

Last, the planner advised her to give gifts of money each year to her children so that the estate taxes at her death would not be as great. If during her lifetime she gave them stock or mutual funds, they would receive her cost basis on them as well. For example, suppose Jean bought Coca-Cola stock in 1987 for $33 a share. Since then Coke has split at least three times, making the cost basis somewhere around $4 a share. Suppose it now sells for about $67 a share. If she or anyone to whom she gifted the stock sold it, they would pay taxes on the capital gains—the difference between her cost ($4) and the current value ($67). If the Coke stock stayed in her estate until she died, the beneficiaries would receive the stock on a "stepped-up basis," meaning the new "cost" would be the value of the stock on Jean's date of death. Where the assets are in stocks or mutual funds that have appreciated in value, it is generally best to keep them in the estate and let them pass to the next generation at the stepped-up basis. It is also a good idea to use stocks with a low basis to give to charities or churches instead of cash.

Jean inherited the Coca-Cola stock we referred to above from her husband. The new basis would be the current market value on the date her husband died, not the $4 original cost. "It would have been hard for me to suggest that she do all of this," John said. "Mom has resisted me every step of the way, and I just take the heat. I listen to her vent. Then I steer her some more. It's hard to do. It's sort of a role reversal. I am the parent and she is like a teenage daughter. She still doesn't trust the planner. She won't say anything when we are in the office, but when we leave, *hold on!* She says, 'I kept quiet for you. You would have crawled under the table if I had protested.'"

There is an additional, ironic, problem. Now that Jean is financially comfortable, she is reluctant to spend her money. "Mom and Dad always scrimped and saved," John said. "They grew up in the depression. She is carrying a lot of baggage left over from those years of frugality. She really doesn't know how to spend her money. I try to help her have a good time with it. 'You can buy this,' I tell her. 'You worked for it!'"

"The elderly need nurturing and direction. They often need help so they cannot be taken advantage of financially. Then they need to be reminded that at this time in their life they can enjoy it a little. Go ahead and spend the money."

Addressing Inheritance Problems

If you have an aging parent with some assets, it is wise to begin thinking about positioning the portfolio to provide both income and some growth to take your parent into his or her advancing years. In addition, you should address the passing of the assets to the next generation while your parent is alive.

John was correct in suggesting that his mother get help with diversifying her portfolio. It is a dilemma, however, if the stocks your parent owns were purchased many years ago and have virtually no cost basis. It is difficult to sell an asset if the tax liability is high.

Fortunately, effective May 1997, the law governing how capital gains are taxed was changed. If an asset was held for more than 18 months, the maximum tax rate will be 20 percent. To compute the profit, use the following formula: Today's current market value minus the cost = profit.

Computing the basis in a stock. If you bought stock, your purchase price is your basis. If someone gave you shares of stock, you must find out what that person paid for the stock and use that cost to compute your profit. For computing tax, the word "cost" is synonymous with "basis."

If someone dies and leaves stock to you under a will, you may use the market value on the date the person died (or six months later, whichever was used for filing the estate tax return) as your basis. That value is most often higher than the cost of the stock to the original owner and is referred to as the "stepped-up basis" under the tax law.

You can now see why we recommended that Jean give her children cash instead of stock. However, the stocks that were in her husband's name that she inherited at the time of his death would have a higher basis at his death than at the time he purchased them. They would have transferred to Jean at the value on his date of death.

Minimizing the Tax Consequences of Estates

If your parents have a big portfolio of stocks with a low basis, the following are several possible things they can do to minimize the tax consequences:

First, encourage your parents to meet charitable gifting commitments by gifting the low-basis stock or mutual fund itself to the charity. Every charity and most all churches have brokerage accounts set up for this purpose. Call the charity or church and ask for its procedure; it will be glad to provide the details. Your action allows you to deduct the current market value of the stock as an itemized deduction on Schedule A of your tax return but neither you nor the charity will have to pay the capital gains tax on it.

Second, engage a tax preparer to help decide how to balance losses with gains as you help your parents decide which stocks to sell and when. Never let a broker or financial planner completely liquidate a portfolio of stocks at once to achieve diversification without consulting your tax preparer.

Third, if there are no losses to offset gains, consider liquidating the stocks over a period of years if at all possible to prevent your parents from creeping up into the next tax bracket.

Fourth, if the portfolio of stocks is quite large and pays inadequate dividends, your parents may wish to consider a charitable remainder annuity trust (CRAT) or a charitable remainder unitrust (CRUT). Under the terms of a CRAT or CRUT, the donor (a parent) may donate shares of stock and receive in return a deduction on his or her tax return for the charitable donation. Inside the trust, your parent may sell the low-basis stock and pay no capital gains tax, allowing the parent-donor to purchase other assets and thus diversify the portfolio to create income.

In addition to being the donor, your parent may also serve as the trustee and be in charge of the trust. Your parent may also be the income beneficiary of the trust. This means that for his or her lifetime, your parent will receive the income generated by the assets in the trust. The major stipulation is that after your parent's death, the charity must receive the principal. Certain complex arrangements allow parents to direct future income to their children. Discuss this with a tax specialist.

The establishment and maintenance of a CRAT or a CRUT is complex. An attorney who specializes in these trusts will need to be consulted. Special rules about income percentages are allowed for each trust and special rules dictate how the charitable deduction is calculated. Your parents will need a good tax preparer to compute the applicable tax deduction.

Because the donated assets of this trust are removed from the estate for good, many people purchase life insurance to replace the assets, an especially good plan for donors in good health.

Another variation to this trust arrangement is giving the heirs the right to receive the income after a parent is gone. If your parent opts for this provision, the charitable deduction for which your parent qualifies is smaller.

Fifth, your parents may wish to give some stock to you or to grandchildren now, thus removing the asset from the estate. If the asset is not producing income and the main goal is to reduce estate taxes, your parents should consider "gifting" to heirs while they are living. No income tax savings are generated from this option—only estate tax savings.

> *"Next to God, thy parents."*
>
> —*William Penn*

WHAT BOOMERS SHOULD BE SURE IS DONE FOR OR BY THEIR PARENTS

To make your life easier in the future, spend some time talking with your aging parents to determine if the following items have been attended to. If not, work with your parents to be sure they are. And, by the way, make sure you attend to these issues in your own situation.

Name a person to whom a health care power of attorney will be given. If one of your parents becomes incapacitated, someone should have permission from that parent to make decisions in the parent's interest. Some families decide the children jointly should have the power of attorney. This is difficult under the best of circumstances if children live in different cities or have a difficult time agreeing on things. It is best for one person to be named.

This is not an expensive project and most lawyers will provide a power of attorney if they draw up the will.

Have your parents read and sign a living will. A living will differs from the health care power of attorney in that it addresses what the medical team should do if life support systems should become necessary. Some people want to be kept alive as long as possible and others don't if they are on a life support system. Your parents will probably have definite opinions that should be written down and signed. Sometimes, a hospital or nursing home in your parents' town has a form they want signed. If they do, it is best to use it.

Have your parents work with the lawyer to develop their wills. A will designates the person—called the executor—who will handle the disposition of their assets after they are gone. If the assets are to be placed in a trust, a trustee must be named to manage the assets. Wills spell out which person(s) receive which assets.

If your parents are willing to discuss it, have them tell you what they want done at their funeral. My father-in-law has put on audio tape exactly what he wants done when he dies. He is not morbid about it; he just thinks it will save us a lot of trouble at a time when we will be grieving and will not want to be thinking about a lot of details. My father has written down his wishes, has prepaid for his and my mother's cemetery plots, and for the opening and closing.

Help your parents decide if the portfolio arrangement is satisfactory to cover their income needs. Many elderly people have plenty of assets but hate to pay taxes when they sell an asset. Therefore, they often sacrifice income just because they don't want to pay taxes necessary to achieve asset balance that would give them more income. If you intervene with a tax preparer, you may be able to help them explore ways to achieve their income goals at the minimum tax level possible.

Checklist for Boomers Caring for Aging Parents

Help parents care for their emotional and physical well-being through steps that include

- making sure they receive inoculations such as flu shots and once-a-lifetime pneumonia shots;

- making sure they go for routine medical checkups;

- making sure they follow the doctor's instructions, including those pertaining to medications;

- encouraging and, if necessary, helping facilitate regular exercise; and

- encouraging and, if necessary, helping facilitate regular social activities.

Help parents get and keep their financial house in order through steps that include

- making sure their principal and purchasing power are protected;

- keeping an up-to-date will and establishing a health care power of attorney and a living will;

- divesting themselves of some of their outdated investments, such as CDs, in favor of investments that will grow over time;

- diversifying their investments; and

- employing strategies that will reduce estate taxes upon their death.

Optimally, aging parents should engage the help of financial planners, tax preparers, and elder law attorneys, who have the expertise to help them avoid many pitfalls.

How to Be a Boomer Millionaire

"My boy," said the millionaire, "when I was your
age, I carried water for a gang of bricklayers."

"I'm mighty proud of you, Father. If it hadn't
been for your pluck and perseverance, I might
have had to do something like that myself."

—*Anonymous from* Public Speakers' Treasure Chest

*B*eing a millionaire was once an impossible dream for most people. However, today the number of people who reach that financial level is steadily rising. According to the Dow Jones News Service, in 1995 there were more than 4.1 million Americans with at least $600,000 in gross assets, up from 3.7 million in 1992. Nearly 1.5 million had a net worth of $1 million or more, the IRS said in its quarterly bulletin on income statistics reported in the *Atlanta Journal Constitution,* March 27, 1998, and available on IRS's Internet site, at http://www.irs.ustreas.gov.

Perhaps you want to be a millionaire. Can you make it? It's entirely possible, and in this short chapter I'll chart the path.

The first question is *why* be a millionaire. Let's look at what $1 million will do for you. You can call yourself "a millionaire," a goal many will never achieve. Perhaps you want to own several houses, travel, and afford the "good life." Maybe you want to pass wealth on to your children. Maybe you want to be financially independent for the rest of your life. Your reasons for wanting a million dollars could be any or all of the above or you may have a completely different reason. In any case, the only thing you need to think about on your journey to millionaire status is how you balance living for today with your goals for the future. After all, no one knows for sure what the future holds so you certainly want to also live for today. But having a million dollars is possible for many with planning and discipline and without sacrificing everything today.

With $1 million, you can invest for growth and income. Invested properly with about 50 percent in stocks and 50 percent in bonds, it will provide you with income that can grow as you age. But not only will your income grow, your principal will also grow over time.

EATING THE FRUIT BUT NOT THE TREES

The new models for retirement planning call for never spending your principal because boomers have a reported average life expectancy of 100 years.

Years ago, our grandparents retired and if they had retirement capital at all, they probably invested it in bonds and withdrew fixed income generated by the interest paid on the bonds. If they didn't die early, they probably began spending their principal, but before they spent it all, many died in their 60s, 70s, or 80s. Today, more and more seniors are living to well into their 80s and 90s.

You may not live to 100, but it is probably safe to say you will probably live longer than your parents and grandparents. If you do, you won't have the luxury of placing your retirement dollars into safe bonds and living on fixed income. Instead, you will have to place at least half of your retirement capital into stocks and hope for their growth as you age. That means you'll have to have some retirement capital subject to the fluctuations of the stock market for as long as you live.

Visualize your retirement capital as a fruit orchard. While you are retired, you want to eat the fruit of your retirement orchard. You would never think of cutting down your fruit trees and eating the tree because next year you'll need more fruit to eat. And if you've cut down the trees, you'll have no fruit.

This analogy is what we mean by investing your money for growth even through retirement. You should place your money into income-producing stocks as well as bonds and spend no more than 7 percent of your principal each year. This will ensure that you never eat your trees and that your trees will still grow for the future.

WANTING $1 MILLION WHEN YOU HAVEN'T YET STARTED ON IT

If you want to be a millionaire and you haven't started yet, I have provided a chart you can use to tell you how much you need to invest at various rates of return in order to reach millionaire status by the year you designate. It's organized by the number of years from retirement that you are making your computation.

First, you must determine how many years from now you want to have a million dollars. Then look at the rates of return I've provided. Choose the rate of return that is realistic for you and will allow your money to grow to $1 million by your target date.

You must then select investments that have demonstrated track records delivering the rate of return you need. Unless you think our stock market will be delivering the same double-digit rates of return we have had in the most recent 15 years, you'll need to choose funds whose performance you can evaluate in those two bad years of 1973–74. You'll want the annual average rate of return, including those two bad years, to be enough to meet your goal. Be sure to find out how the track record was created. If it was created by one person (we call that the "star" approach) or by a series of people ("stars"), you can't be as confident that the past returns are even remotely similar to returns that will be realized in the future. Check back to Chapter 7 for a set of criteria you can use to select a mutual fund managed by a system approach dating back to 1973. While there are no guarantees, a systems approach provides some hope that returns of the past might be replicated in the future, admittedly not guaranteed.

Once you have selected your investment vehicle providing growth or aggressive growth, use Figure 11.1 to determine how much you must set aside to reach your goal. The best way to stay on goal is to determine how much you have to invest every month and have the fund company deduct that amount from your checking or savings account automatically on an appointed day. Now take action and we'll see you after you've become a millionaire!

**FIGURE 11.1   Retirement Builder: Saving Monthly for a
$1 Million Nest Egg**

Years from Retirement	Monthly Amount (10% rate of return)	Monthly Amount (12% rate of return)	Monthly Amount (14% rate of return)
9	$5,698	$5,133	$4,613
10	4,841	4,304	3,815
11	4,152	3,641	3,182
12	3,588	3,103	2,673
13	3,119	2,660	2,258
14	2,726	2,291	1,916
15	2,392	1,982	1,632
16	2,108	1,720	1,394
17	1,863	1,497	1,194
18	1,651	1,306	1,025
19	1,467	1,142	881
20	1,306	1,001	760
21	1,165	878	655
22	1,040	772	566
23	931	679	489
24	834	598	423
25	747	527	367
26	671	465	317
27	602	410	275
28	542	363	239
29	487	320	207
30	439	283	180

APPENDIX A

What History Tells Us about Our Financial Future

*W*hen one discovers the past performance of Treasuries, corporate and government bonds, and the S&P 500 index by studying the Ibbotson bar charts in this appendix, several conclusions can be drawn.

First, we have had inflation in this country since 1954 and are likely to experience it for many years to come. Therefore, we must protect the purchasing power of our income as we move into the future by making sure the returns we receive are greater than inflation, which has averaged 3.2 percent a year since 1926.

Second, Treasuries have only averaged 3.8 percent a year since 1926. If you subtract the average inflation of 3.2 percent from 3.8 percent, you have an excess return of .6 percent. That means if you have $100,000 in your retirement nest egg and wish to reinvest the percentage needed to cover inflation and spend the rest, you'll have $600 a year for each $100,000 you have to cover your cost of living.

This is why interest-bearing investment vehicles are said to "barely keep up with inflation."

Third, corporate and government bonds have averaged returns of 6.1 percent and 5.6 percent, respectively, since 1926. Again subtracting the average inflation of 3.2 percent, you would have about 2.9 to 2.4 percent to support your cost of living. Using our $100,000 nest egg example above, you would have between $2,400 and $2,900 a year to spend for each $100,000 in your nest egg. Furthermore, the interest paid by bonds does not increase over time. It is fixed and paid every six months.

It might surprise you that in some years bonds have actually produced negative returns as shown in the bar chart of bonds' historical returns. The reason for the fluctuation is that if investors had sold their bonds during a negative return year to purchase stocks or Treasuries, the investors would have received less money than the bonds cost the year before. The only condition under which bonds retain their value is if investors hold them till maturity and the company or government issuing the bond is still in existence to pay investors their principal.

Fourth, everyone knows investments in stocks can go up but can also go down. Does it surprise you to see the negative bars in the bond bar chart? Perhaps you didn't realize the risks associated with investing in bonds. In spite of the risks in buying bonds, the potential losses in stocks are greater.

The S&P 500 bar chart reports the fluctuations of the Fortune 500 stocks beginning in 1926. Study the chart. Look for the two consecutive years during which the S&P 500 declined the most. You'll find the most devastating two consecutive years were 1930–31 when the market dropped 68 percent. These were the two worst years of the Great Depression.

Now find the next two worst consecutive years. They were 1973–74 when the performance decline was 41 percent. If investors had remained invested for seven years after the 1930–31 decline and four years after the 1973–74 decline, they would have gotten all their money back.

Notice also that the average annual returns since 1926 in the S&P 500 have been 10.8 percent per year. Many say a "normal" market downturn is 10 percent. We haven't had a "normal" market correction of 10 percent since 1974, which is why experts say we are living in the greatest bull market our country has ever known.

Fifth, over time, investment performances change from asset class to asset class. If you want to achieve growth in excess of inflation, you'll need to have at least some of your investments in stocks. The greater your need for income, the greater your need for bonds in your portfolio.

Sixth, investing in mutual funds instead of in a narrow portfolio of individual stocks is the preferred way to invest. In years past a person could purchase a stock and pay for it, get the money to the broker within five days. Trading then progressed at a pace that seemed fast at the time but in comparison with the pace of trading today, yesterday's trading speed was a snail's pace. Today, a mutual fund or pension fund manager can press a key on the computer minutes before the market closes and buy or sell, not a hundred or a thousand shares of a stock, but several million. Lone investors holding 100 or 1,000 shares can be adversely affected by large-volume trades and find themselves waiting years to recover a loss created by a single large-volume trade initiated by a single manager.

It is best in today's world for small investors to hire a mutual fund manager to manage their money so that even the smallest investors can be part of trades of several million shares at a fraction of the cost.

Examine the bar charts that follow to learn about the year-by-year fluctuations of each asset class of investments available to you through mutual funds.

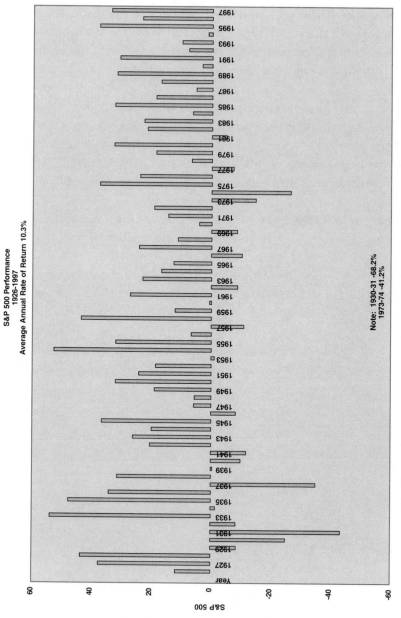

S&P 500 Performance
1926-1997
Average Annual Rate of Return 10.3%

Note: 1930-31 -68.2%
1973-74 -41.2%

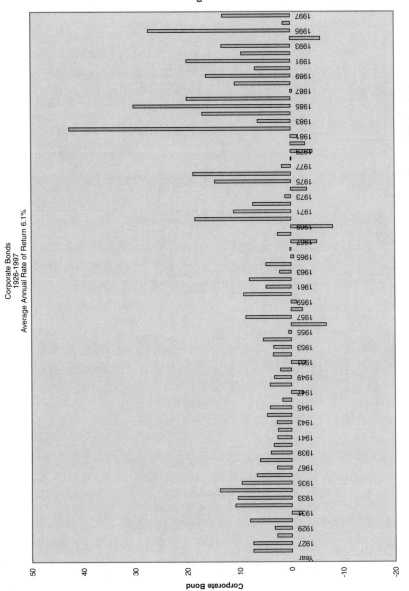

Corporate Bonds
1926-1997
Average Annual Rate of Return 6.1%

☐ Corporate Bonds

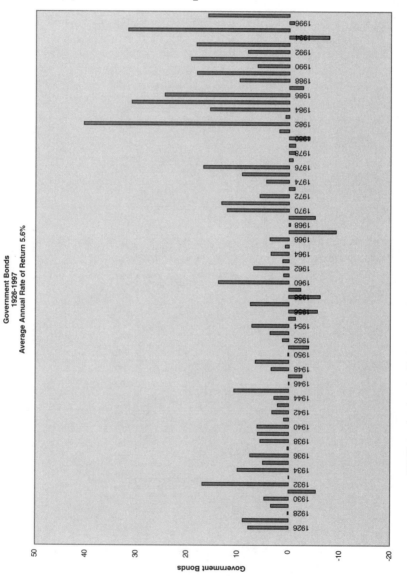

Government Bonds
1926-1997
Average Annual Rate of Return 5.6%

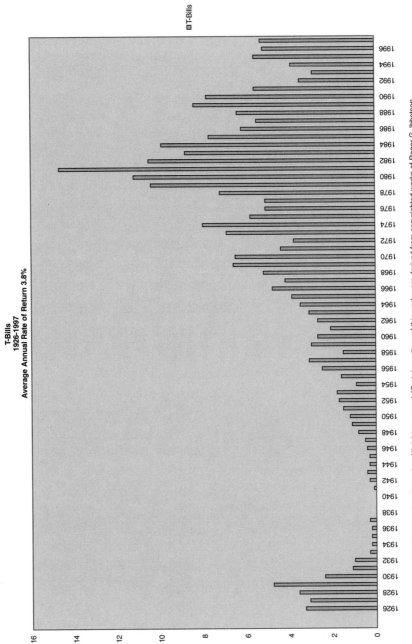

T-Bills
1926-1997
Average Annual Rate of Return 3.8%

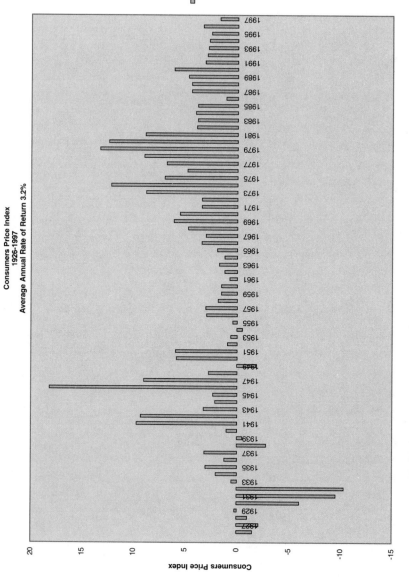

Consumers Price Index
1926-1997
Average Annual Rate of Return 3.2%

☐ Consumers Price Index

APPENDIX B

Household and Family Expense Worksheet

Expense Categories	Current Monthly Total	Retirement Monthly Total
1. Home *(Mortgage payment, insurance, tax, improvements, yard)*	_____	_____
2. Utilities *(gas, power, water, cable, phone)*	_____	_____
3. Food *(groceries, restaurants)*	_____	_____
4. Recreation/Entertainment *(vacations, clubs, concerts, etc.)*	_____	_____

5. Automobile   _____   _____
   (payments, gas, repairs, etc.)

6. Medical   _____   _____
   (Doctor, drugs, insurance, etc.)

7. Donations/Gifts   _____   _____
   (charities, church, birthdays,
       holidays)

8. Savings/Investments   _____   _____
   (savings, reserves, investments,
       education funding)

9. Life insurance   _____   _____
   (personal, life, disability)

10. Personal necessities   _____   _____
    (hair, cosmetics, laundry,
        subscriptions)

11. Clothing   _____   _____
    (shoes, alterations, cleaning,
        etc.)

12. Depreciating assets   _____   _____
    (major purchases)

13. Pets   _____   _____
    (vet bills, prescriptions,
        grooming, etc.)

14. Children's/Parents' expenses   _____   _____
    (parties, medicines, etc.)

15. Miscellaneous   _____   _____

   Total (Monthly)   _____   _____

   Total (Annually)   _____   _____

APPENDIX C

Withdrawing Income from Retirement Funds Penalty-Free

*I*nternal Revenue Code (IRC) section 72(t)(1) imposes an additional 10 percent tax on amounts withdrawn from retirement plans (including IRAs) prior to the owner's reaching age 59½. However, IRC section 72(t)(2)(A)(iv) provides that this tax does *not* apply to distributions that are part of a series of substantially equal periodic payments (not less frequently than annually) made over the life expectancy of the planholder or the joint life expectancies of the planholder and his or her beneficiary. Some specific provisions of this section are as follows:

- Once a series of payments is begun, it cannot be modified before either

  – age 59½ or
  – five years from the date the payments began, whichever happens last.

- Payments are considered to be substantially equal periodic payments if the amount to be distributed is computed using one of the following three methods:

  1. The account balance is divided by the planholder's life expectancy or joint life expectancy from IRS tables.
  2. The account balance is amortized at a reasonable interest rate over the planholder's life expectancy or joint expectancy from IRS tables.
  3. The account balance is amortized at a reasonable interest rate over the planholder's life expectancy from an insurance mortality table. In this method there is no provision for using joint life expectancy.

- If it is determined by the IRS that these provisions have not been satisfied, the planholder will have to pay a tax that would have been imposed under section 72(t)(1), plus interest, for the amounts withdrawn which did not qualify under section 72(t)(2)(A)(iv).

Adapted from *1997 U.S. Master Tax Guide,* CCH Incorporated, Chicago, 1996.

APPENDIX D

Estate Tax Rate Schedule

Column A Taxable amount over (in dollars)	Column B Table amount not over (in dollars)	Column C Tax on amount in column A (in dollars)	Column D Rate of tax on excess over amount in column A (Percent)
0	10,000	0	18
10,000	20,000	1,800	20
20,000	40,000	3,800	22
40,000	60,000	8,200	24
60,000	80,000	13,000	26
80,000	100,000	18,200	28
100,000	150,000	23,800	30
150,000	250,000	38,800	32
250,000	500,000	70,800	34
500,000	750,000	155,800	37
750,000	1,000,000	248,300	39
1,000,000	1,250,000	345,800	41
1,250,000	1,500,000	448,300	43
1,500,000	2,000,000	555,800	45
2,000,000	2,500,000	780,800	49
2,500,000	3,000,000	1,025,800	53
3,000,000	. . . .	1,290,800	55

Source: *1998 U.S. Master Tax Guide,* CCH Incorporated, Chicago, 1997.

APPENDIX E

Resources for Finding a Financial Planner

*T*he Institute of Certified Financial Planners, based in Denver, is the professional organization that represents more than 12,000 certified financial planners as of June 30, 1998, from coast to coast. Members must maintain their certification through the completion of continuing education requirements. To contact the organization, call 800-282-7526.

The International Association for Financial Planning (IAFP) is the membership organization for financial planners. According to its 1996 internal survey, it has 15,744 members. The average member is 48 years old and has been a member for five years. Only 4,000 have been members for more than eight years. Twenty percent are women. Almost 40 percent are CFPs, 20 percent are chartered life underwriters (CLUs), and 6 percent are CPAs. About 32 percent are paid through a combination of fees and commissions, about 20 percent are salaried, 13 percent are commission-based only, and only 7.2 percent are fee only. To contact the organization, call 800-945-4237.

Members of the National Association of Personal Financial Advisers include financial advisers who charge a fee for their advice and collect no commissions from sales of investments. To contact the association, call 800-366-2732.

INDEX

ABOUT THE AUTHOR

*K*ay Retta Shirley, Ph.D., does more than tell people how to invest their hard-earned money, she also teaches them how to make their assets last a lifetime. Her first book, *Live Long & Profit: Wealthbuilding Strategies for Every Stage of Your Life* (Dearborn Financial Publishing), gives people of all income levels the knowledge they need to become millionaires when they retire.

Dr. Shirley, a former teacher, is president of Financial Development Corporation, as well as a registered representative, registered principal, and branch manager for Titan Value Equities Group, Inc., a nationwide association of independent financial planners. Titan is a broker-dealer and a member of the NASD and SIPC. Financial Development Corporation is a Registered Investment Adviser with the State of Georgia.

The news media seek her views on many topics, including the ups and downs of the stock market and the fundamentals of financial planning. The October 1998 issue of *Entrepreneur* magazine profiled her book *Live Long & Profit.* She has been interviewed on CNN, CNNfn, Fox News Channel, and Lifetime TV. She also has been quoted in the *Atlanta Journal-Constitution,* the *Atlanta Business Chronicle,* and *Inc.* magazine. For two years, Dr. Shirley delivered the daily "Free Advice" financial segment of WAGA-TV's *Good Day Atlanta.* She has made appearances on Georgia Public TV and created the show *Moneytalk* for Atlanta's WGNX-TV.

In the 1980s, Dr. Shirley was included on lists of Atlanta's Top Twenty-Seven Self-Made Women, Atlanta's Fourteen Women on Top, and Atlanta's Top Women Executives. The *Atlanta Business Chronicle* named her one of Ten Key Decision-Makers in Buckhead in 1990. She has served on the board of directors of the 1,000-member Buckhead Business Association since 1984, becoming the group's first woman president in 1989. She was a founding member of the Buckhead Club and belongs to the Women's Commerce Club.

Dr. Shirley hosts financial seminars and often speaks to civic, community, and religious groups. In 1991, she shared conference agendas with *Wall Street Week* host Louis Rukeyser, then-General Norman Schwarzkopf, and Dr. Joyce Brothers. In 1990, BellSouth added her to the list of approved financial planners for its key managers. She was also a management consultant for large engineering and medical organizations from 1975 to 1980. She is a member of the Georgia Society of the Institute of Certified Financial Planners and is a member of the International Association for Financial Planning. She also is a licensed life, health, and disability insurance agent.

She earned her B.S. in mathematics from Mississippi State University and a Ph.D. in educational administration and management from Georgia State University. Georgia State University named her one of its 24 Outstanding Alumni in 1989 and asked her to serve on its alumni board in 1997 and 1998.

Dr. Shirley practices what she preaches and recommends only investments in which she is personally invested.